THIRD EDITION

Bicycling
the Backroads
=OF SOUTHWEST WASHINGTON=

By Erin and Bill Woods

Cartoons by Dale Martin
The Mountaineers, Seattle

The Mountaineers: Organized 1906
"...to explore, study, preserve and enjoy
the natural beauty of the Northwest."

6 5 4
6 5 4 3

Published by The Mountaineers
1011 Klickitat Way, Seattle, Washington 98134

Published simultaneously in Canada by Douglas & McIntyre, Ltd.
1615 Venables Street, Vancouver, British Columbia, V5L 2H1

Published simultaneously in Great Britain by Cordee,
3a De Montfort Street, Leicester, England, LE1 7HD

Manufactured in the United States of America

Edited by Ramona Gault
Cover design by Judy Petry
Maps by Helen Sherman and Bill Woods
Cartoons by Dale Martin

Cover Photograph: Boston Harbor on South Puget Sound
Photo By Kirkendall/Spring

Library of Congress Cataloging in Publication Data
Woods, Erin
    Bicycling the backroads of southwest Washington.

    Includes indexes.
    1. Bicycle touring — Washington (State) — Guide-books.
2. Cycling paths — Washington (State) — Guide-books.
3. Washington (State) — Description and travel — 1994 —
Guide-books.   I. Woods, Bill.   II. Title.
GV1045.5.W2W67   917.9704'43   80-14682
ISBN 0-89886-390-2

NOTE ABOUT RIDE NUMBERING

Do not look for missing pages. The tours in this book start at number 94 to follow in sequence those in *Bicycling the Backroads Around Puget Sound* and *Bicycling the Backroads of Northwest Washington*. Seattle, WA: The Mountaineers. This numbering system was adopted to facilitate cross-referencing and compilation using tours from all three books. Tours numbered 1 to 54, when cited, refer to the first title, and tours 55 to 93, when cited, refer to the second title.

CONTENTS

LOCATION OF TOURS BY NUMBER

4

MAP LEGEND

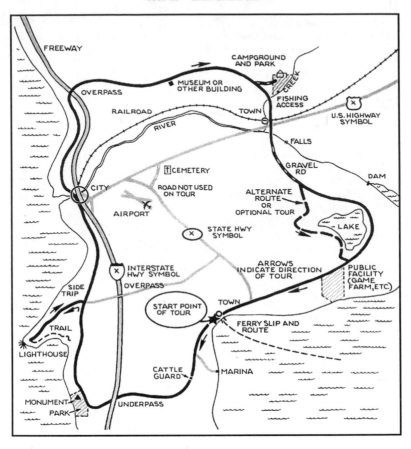

INTRODUCTION

The resurgence in the 1970s of the bicycle as a recreational and transportation vehicle has encouraged the start of what is hoped will be a network of bicycle routes and trails in western Washington. The Burke-Gilman Trail, from Gas Works Park in Seattle to Bothell Landing Park in Bothell, although vigorously opposed in its planning stages by adjoining landowners, is now a coveted and highly popular recreational facility as well as a commuter route for University of Washington students. The Sammamish River Trail, from Redmond to Bothell, has become very popular and is now linked with Burke-Gilman for a continuous trail of over 20 miles. The Interurban Park Trail, from Tukwila to Pacific on the Pierce County line, also attracts many cyclists, and periodical improvements have been added to remove the detours and extend its length.

Urban trail systems, however, are often heavily occupied and as a result present an element of danger. The accident rate per mile can be significantly higher than the rate on adjacent roadways, and cyclists must be constantly on the alert to avoid colliding with other trail users, including beginning cyclists, joggers, roller skaters, dogs, equestrians, and parents pushing baby strollers.

Once having acquired a degree of cycling proficiency, most bicyclists prefer to tour on quiet backroads. Although in Washington State such roads have a high degree of connectivity, there are several areas where only busy highways offer a reasonable means of passage. Progress is being made

"This says to turn left."

here, too, with the opening to bicyclists of interstate highway shoulders throughout the state, with only urban areas excluded. On secondary highways, upgrading of design to federal standards provides paved shoulders for cyclists to ride comfortably out of the automotive traffic pattern.

The Washington State Department of Wildlife, which has jurisdiction over the state's fishing and hunting access areas, has marked many of these convenient stopping areas as conservation parks, requiring users to have a current fishing, hunting, or conservation license. In particular, Tour 104 in this book begins at one of these marked areas. Other routes that may require a license for use of rest areas are Tours 98, 120, 122, 123, 135, and 138. Before starting on any one of the above tours, purchase of a conservation or equivalent game license is recommended.

For many years, two primary alternatives for overnighting bicycle tourists have been low-cost campgrounds and higher-cost motels. Campgrounds often are dominated by noisy recreational vehicle occupants, and shower facilities may leave something to be desired. Motels are sterile, impersonal institutions and may be rather expensive for the solo cyclist. Now there is another alternative represented by the increasing number of bed-and-breakfast (B & B) opportunities in Washington State. Finding out about them, however, may not be easy. Some are listed in local telephone directories, some advertise in tourist magazines or are registered with listing agencies, and many depend on word-of-mouth promotion. To assist bicyclists in taking advantage of this new opportunity, a listing is provided of B & B telephone numbers and locations in the index of this book. Some have been checked out by the authors; many have not.

Aside from this, you are on your own. Ride safely and enjoy your touring.

Erin and Bill Woods

SAFETY CONSIDERATIONS

Safety is an important concern in all outdoor activities. No guidebook can alert you to every hazard or anticipate the limitations of every reader, so the descriptions in this book are not representations that a particular trip is safe for your party. When you take a trip, you assume responsibility for your own safety. Some of the trips described in this book may require you to do no more than look both ways before crossing the street; on others, more attention to safety may be required due to terrain, traffic, weather, the capabilities of your party, or other factors. Keeping informed on current conditions and exercising common sense are the keys to a safe, enjoyable outing. On all trips, be sure to wear a helmet and urge your companions to do so as well.

The Mountaineers

KITSAP AND PIERCE COUNTIES

94 SOUTHWORTH–GIG HARBOR– KOPACHUCK STATE PARK

STARTING POINT: Southworth ferry terminal. From I-5 in Seattle take exit 163 or 163A (Spokane Street and West Seattle). Cross Duwamish Waterway to West Seattle, climb hill, and at traffic signal continue through on Fauntleroy Avenue (follow Vashon ferry signs). Park in Lincoln Park (north parking lot) 3 blocks north of Fauntleroy ferry terminal. Take bicycles on ferry to Southworth. From I-5 in Tacoma, take exit 132 (State Route 16) and follow across Narrows Bridge to Kitsap Peninsula. Turn right on Sedgwick Road 14 miles north of bridge and follow to Southworth ferry terminal parking lot.

DISTANCE: 35 to 51 miles.
TERRAIN: Strenuous hills.
TOTAL CUMULATIVE ELEVATION GAIN: 2300 to 3100 feet.
RECOMMENDED TIME OF YEAR: Any season.
RECOMMENDED STARTING TIME: 8 to 10 A.M. from Southworth ferry terminal.
ALLOW: 6 to 8 hours; 1 day or overnight.
POINTS OF INTEREST
Gig Harbor shops
Kopachuck State Park

ELEVATION PROFILE

DISTANCE IN MILES

The Southworth–Port Orchard route (Tour 44) has long been a favorite of cycle-touring Seattle residents for its close-in starting point, beautiful scenery, easy hills, and moderate traffic. The tour described here shares all but one of these virtues, the difference being the hills. The eastern edge of southern Kitsap Peninsula presents a high bluff cut by several stream channels, making many ups and downs in the roads. This should not deter a determined cyclist, however, as the tour may be shortened at will, to almost any length or degree of effort, by taking advantage of short crossroads that cut the course at frequent intervals.

The scenery, although offering few seascapes, is nonetheless delightful for viewing cool, green forest, upland lakes and valleys, and occasional deep coves and bays. White pine and madrona vary the usual sights of fir, hemlock, and alder of second-growth forests, with evergreen huckleberry, sword fern, and oceanspray filling in the understory. The upland lakes have shallow slopes supporting dense growths of water lilies. In the estuarial coves, great blue herons vie with ducks, grebes, and gulls for their share of aquatic tidbits.

Gig Harbor has developed a handicraft orientation, and its stores are favored by shoppers looking for unusual arts and crafts. Several restaurants and cafes offer a variety of fare.

By using Kopachuck State Park as an overnight stop, the touring cyclist

9

can test bicycle camping gear close to home before setting out on longer trips. Hot showers, secluded campsites, and waterside picnic shelters make this one of Washington State's better-appointed parks. A group camp area is available by reservation with the park manager. A boat anchorage with nearby rest rooms and showers caters to marine visitors.

MILEAGE LOG

0.0 Southworth ferry terminal. Head uphill on **State Route 160**.

0.3 Turn left on **Sedgwick Road** and head uphill.

2.8 Turn left on **Banner Road** as Sedgwick tops a summit. Dip down, cross Fragaria Creek, and climb out again at mile 5.9. Views of Colvos Passage and Point Defiance at mile 8.1. Descend steep, curving hill to Olalla on the shores of Puget Sound.

9.2 Turn left on **Crescent Valley Road** by Olalla store as Olalla Valley Road goes right. Wind up out of the valley. Road changes name to **Crescent Valley Drive N.W.** as it enters Pierce County at mile 11.6.

15.7 Turn right on **96th Street N.W.** toward Gig Harbor and Tacoma. City park on right at bottom of hill at mile 15.9; picnic lunch stop.

16.1 Turn left on **Harborview Drive** in Gig Harbor as Vernhardson Road continues up a steep hill. *Note: Short tour turns sharp right on Peacock Hill Avenue at 16.5 and picks up mileage log at 32.2.* Continue left with Harborview around harbor. Cafe at 17.6.

17.8 Turn right on **Pioneer Way** at blinking red light as Harborview angles left. Crank up steep hill. Cross State Route 16 on overpass at mile 18.5. Road changes name to **Wollochet Drive N.W.** and winds down to tip of Wollochet Bay.

20.8 Turn right on **Artondale Drive N.W.** as Wollochet bends left along bay. Road is renamed **78th Avenue N.E.** and **Whitmore Drive N.W.**

23.9 Turn left at stop sign as Ray Nash Drive N.W. joins from the right.

25.0 Continue straight toward Kopachuck State Park on **Artondale Drive N.W.** Arletta store is 1.0 mile to the left. 56 Street N.W. goes left into Kopachuck State Park at mile 26.0 as Artondale Drive changes name to **Kopachuck Drive N.W.** *Note: State park is a possible overnight stop; see text for facilities.*

27.6 Cross a small inlet and continue on **Ray Nash Drive** as it enters from the right. Small grocery here.

28.3 Turn right toward State Route 16 on **Rosedale Street N.W.** and climb a long hill. Enter Gig Harbor at mile 30.8. Observe 25-mph speed limit as road dives down a steep hill.

31.3 Turn left at stop sign on **Stinson Avenue**.

31.5 Go straight on **Harborview Drive** as Stinson ends and follow Harborview to the right around the harbor.

32.2 Turn left on **Peacock Hill Avenue**. Enter Kitsap County at mile 36.7.

37.7 Turn right on **S.E. Nelson Road** as Peacock ends.

38.0 Turn left on **Fagerud Road S.E.**, which executes two bends and descends hill.

39.1 Turn right on **S.E. Olalla-Burley Road** as Fagerud ends.

39.5 Turn left on **Wallace Road S.E.** then bear left on **Olalla Valley Road**

by Olalla Food Center.

42.2   Turn left on **S.E. Mullenix Road** toward Port Orchard, Bremerton, and Tacoma.

42.4   Turn right on **Long Lake Road S.E.** as Mullenix starts down a long hill. Cycle past Long Lake.

44.9   Turn right at wye on **Lake Valley Road S.E.** as Long Lake Road turns left. Road bends left again shortly.

45.6   Turn right on **S.E. Sedgwick Road** as Mayvolt Road S.E. goes on.

45.8   Turn left on **Locker Road S.E.** Start down long hill at 46.1.

47.5   Turn right on **State Route 160** as Locker ends at bottom of hill.

48.5   Turn left on **Cornell Street**, marked Dead End. Continue along water.

49.1   Go around vehicle barrier in Harper and continue on **State Route 160**.

49.5   Turn left on **Olympiad Road** as shoreline swings left. Follow **Olympiad Drive** left at 49.9 as Nokomis Road goes right.

50.4   Turn left on **S.E. Cherry Street** as Olympiad is marked Dead End.

50.8   Turn left on **State Route 160** toward ferry landing in Southworth.

51.1   Southworth ferry terminal; end of tour.

95 SOUTHWORTH–LONGBRANCH–GIG HARBOR

STARTING POINT: Southworth ferry terminal. From I-5 in Seattle take exit 163 or 163A (Spokane Street and West Seattle). Cross Duwamish Waterway to West Seattle, climb hill, and at traffic signal continue through on Fauntleroy Avenue (follow Vashon ferry signs). Park on side streets uphill from Fauntleroy ferry terminal. Take bicycles on ferry to Southworth. From I-5 in Tacoma, take exit 132 (State Route 16) and follow across Narrows Bridge to Kitsap Peninsula. Turn right on State Route 160 (Sedgwick Road) 14 miles north of bridge and follow to Southworth ferry terminal parking lot.

DISTANCE: Total, 107 miles: first day, 42 miles; second day, 37 miles; third day, 28 miles.
TERRAIN: Hilly.
TOTAL CUMULATIVE ELEVATION GAIN: 6800 feet: first day, 2200 feet; second day, 2700 feet; third day, 1900 feet.

RECOMMENDED TIME OF YEAR: Any season.
RECOMMENDED STARTING TIME: 9 A.M. from Southworth ferry terminal.
ALLOW: 3 days.
POINTS OF INTEREST
Seascapes between Southworth and Port Orchard
Manchester State Park
Penrose Point State Park
Minter Creek Salmon Hatchery
Kopachuck State Park
Gig Harbor shops

Seattleites have often asked for an overnight or multi-day tour that travels over low-traffic roads, has reasonably short mileages, and starts from the Seattle area. Specifications such as these sound nearly impossible to meet, yet this tour does come close. In its short span of 100 miles or so, it offers a wide variety of scenery: the salty seascapes along Puget Sound, frequented by migrating waterfowl of many varieties (ducks, geese, grebes, loons, scoters, and murres, to name a few); inlets from the sound punctuating the forest scenery, pointing long fingers up creek estuaries; forests of alder, maple, fir, hemlock, and cedar, as well as stands of white and lodgepole pine; and the plateau area, with upland lakes, creek valleys, and dairy farms.

There is variety in the towns, too. Harper, Manchester, Point Fosdick, and Longbranch all offered ferry service to the mainland at one time or another but now are sleepy little communities tucked away in out-of-the-way places, their old piers gradually crumbling with decay. Port Orchard still has passenger ferry service to Bremerton and the naval shipyards and has grown to be a thriving city. Conversely, Gig Harbor caters to boaters and tourists with its handsome marina and many small arts and crafts shops.

Camping accommodations at Penrose and Kopachuck state parks include the usual automobile-oriented campsites secluded among trees and shrubbery around a campground loop road and rest rooms with coin-operated hot showers for a welcome clean-up opportunity. Picnic shelters shed the rain in inclement weather. For group outings, both parks have group camp areas, available by reservation with the park manager.

Although much of the tour is through rural country, food is available at convenient points in the itinerary. On the first day, the restaurants and fast-food shops in Port Orchard offer a wide choice of fare. The restaurant in Home is an option for dinner, or perhaps the chowder house in Longbranch. For the second day, the Home restaurant is open for breakfast, and Purdy is convenient for lunch. Two small grocery stores not far from Kopachuck State Park may be visited for dinner materials. On the third day, Gig Harbor is close enough for breakfast, and if a morning of sightseeing and shopping is desired, then lunch there is in order as well. A pleasant city park along Crescent Lake Creek in Gig Harbor may be enjoyed with a picnic lunch. From here the end of the tour is only a few hours away, and cycle tourists may board a ferry for home without a care for the long lines of weekend or holiday automotive traffic. Even with the many hills on this ride, it is a good multi-day tour from Seattle's metropolitan area.

MILEAGE LOG

FIRST DAY

0.0 Southworth ferry terminal. Head west and uphill on **State Route 160**.

0.3 Turn right on **Cherry Street** by gas station just up the hill from ferry terminal.

0.7 Turn right on **Olympiad Drive**, keeping right as Nokomis intersects at mile 1.2.

1.6 Turn right at stop sign at T junction.

2.0 Go around barrier and continue along waterfront on **Cornell Street** in Harper as thoroughfare turns left and starts uphill.

2.5 Turn right at T junction on thoroughfare for 1.0 mile of traffic.

3.5 Turn right on **Yukon Harbor Drive** and descend to waterfront again.

4.4 Bear right on **Colchester Drive** into Manchester.

5.9 Turn left at stop sign on **Main Street** in Manchester. Crank up steep hill one block, then turn right on **Beach Drive**. Side road to Manchester State Park at mile 7.8.

13.1 Bear right on **Bay Street** in Port Orchard at flashing red light. Cafes, fast-food shops in Port Orchard along Bay Street. Cross Sydney Avenue at traffic light at mile 13.6.

14.1 Turn left on **Port Orchard Boulevard** and start uphill.

15.1 Turn right at stop sign at top of hill on **Tremont Street** as Port Orchard Boulevard ends.

15.3 Turn left on **Pottery Avenue**. Go under State Route 16 at mile 16.3. Road name changes to **Sidney Road**.

16.8 Turn right on **Glenwood Road** and cycle into forest.

17.7 Turn right at stop sign with Glenwood Road as Sedgwick Road goes left.

18.8 Continue straight on **Lake Flora Road** toward Clavinwood and Wye Lake as Glenwood Road goes left to Camp Niwana. Road name changes to **Dickinson Road S.W.** at mile 21.8, and to **Carney Lake Road S.W.** at mile 24.7.

29.1 Turn right toward Allyn on **State Route 302**. Busy traffic, narrow shoulder.

29.7 Turn left on **Bliss Cochrane Road KPN** by health-care facility.

31.6 Turn left on **Bay View Road KPN**.

31.9 Turn right on **Van Slyke Road KPN**, then left on **Hall Road KPN** as Van Slyke ends.

32.5 Turn right on **South Vaughn Road KPN** by Key Peninsula Civic Center in Vaughn. Cross inlet at end of Vaughn Bay.

32.9 Bear left and uphill on **Lackey Road KPN** as South Vaughn Road goes right.

36.1 Bear right on **Key Peninsula Highway KPN**. Restaurant on left at mile 37.9, grocery at mile 38.1.

38.3 Turn left on **Hoff Road KPS** just after crossing bridge over tip of Van Geldern Cove. Road is renamed **Lorenz Road KPS**.

40.2 Continue on **Delano Road KPS** as it enters from the right by Lake Bay Marina and grocery.

41.0 Turn left on **158th Avenue KPS** toward Penrose Point State Park, turning left toward camping area as road forks.

41.7 Campground area, Penrose Point State Park.

SECOND DAY

0.0 Campground area of Penrose Point State Park. Head out entrance road, which becomes **158th Avenue KPS** as it leaves the park.

0.6 Turn left on **Delano Road KPS**, which bends right after 0.4 mile and is renamed **142nd Avenue KPS**, and finally **24th Street KPS**.

3.3 Turn left on **158th Avenue KPS** as 24th Street ends. Road name changes to **Reeves Road KPS** and finally **40th Street KPS**.

4.6 Turn left on **Key Peninsula Highway KPS** as 40th Street ends. Longbranch Mercantile and marina at mile 5.4.

7.0 Turn right on **76th Street KPS** as Key Peninsula Highway is marked Dead End. Road name changes to **Whiteman Road KPS** at 9.8. Whiteman Cove Road KPS goes left to Whiteman Cove at mile 10.6.

13.4 Bear left at stop sign on **Key Peninsula Highway KPS**. Pass restaurant at mile 14.9.

20.1 Turn right on **Cramer Road KPN** at flashing amber light in Key Center by cafe and grocery. YMCA Camp Seymour on right at mile 21.1, just after road crosses tip of Glen Cove.

22.7 Turn right on **Creviston Drive KPN** as S.R. 302 appears ahead. Minter Creek Salmon Hatchery on left at mile 23.6.

25.6 Bear right toward Gig Harbor on **State Route 302** and endure traffic for 0.8 mile.

26.4 Turn left on **Goldman Drive N.W.** as S.R. 302 bends right.

27.1 Turn left again on **State Route 302** and cross tip of Carr Inlet on causeway with wide, paved shoulder. *Note: Turning left on Goodrich Drive N.W. just before S.R. 302 crosses causeway and following Pine Road, Bethel-Burley Road, and Burley-Olalla Road to Olalla Valley Road (third-day route) shortens the tour by one day and 22 miles. See maps, pages 15 and 17.*

28.1 Bear right through business area in Purdy at junction of S.R. 302 with Purdy Drive. Cross Purdy Drive at 28.2 and continue on **Goodnough Drive N.W.** Cross Purdy Drive again at mile 29.0 and continue on **Burnham Drive N.W.**

29.9 Turn right on **Woodhill Drive N.W.**, which turns a corner after 0.7 mile and is renamed **70th Avenue N.W.**

31.6 Turn right on **Sehmel Drive N.W.** at stop sign.

32.1 Turn left on **78th Avenue N.W.** at top of hill. As it bottoms out and bends right the road is renamed **Chapman Drive N.W.**, and then **96th Street N.W.**

33.0 Left turn on **86th Avenue N.W.** as 96th Street is marked Dead End. Road bends left at mile 34.0 and is renamed **Rosedale Street N.W.**

34.3 Turn right on **Ray Nash Drive N.W.**

35.0 Continue straight on **Kopachuck Drive N.W.** toward Kopachuck State Park as Ray Nash Drive bends left by small grocery.

36.6 Right turn on **56th Street N.W.** into Kopachuck State Park. Camping area on the right 0.1 mile down the hill.

THIRD DAY

0.0 Entrance to campground area of Kopachuck State Park. Head uphill out of park on **56th Street N.W.**

0.1 Turn right on **Artondale Drive N.W.**

1.0 Turn left on **Ray Nash Drive N.W.** as Artondale Drive ends.

2.3 Turn right on **Whitmore Drive N.W.**, which bends after 1.2 miles and is renamed **78th Avenue N.W.** and finally **Artondale Drive N.W.**

5.2 Turn left on **Wollochet Drive N.W.** at T junction. Cross State Route 16 on overpass at mile 7.4. As it enters Gig Harbor, road dives down steep hill and is renamed **Pioneer Way.** Observe 25-mph speed limit.

8.2 Turn left at flashing red light at bottom of hill on **Harborview Drive.** Follow Harborview along waterfront; cafe. Marina park with public rest rooms on the right at mile 8.3.

9.7 Turn right on **96th Street N.W.** City park on left at 10.0.

10.2 Turn left on **Crescent Valley Drive N.W.** Enter Kitsap County at mile 15.2.

17.4 Bear left on **Olalla Valley Road** by Olalla grocery and post office.

23.3 Turn left on **Banner Road** as Olalla Valley Road ends.

25.2 Turn right on **Sedgwick Road (State Route 160)** as Banner ends.

27.7 Turn right with State Route 160 as Sedgwick ends.

27.8 Southworth ferry terminal; end of ride.

KING COUNTY

96   KENT–PACIFIC

STARTING POINT: City of Kent's Russell Road Park. Take exit 149 (State Route 516) from I-5 and follow State Route 516 down the hill toward Kent. Turn left on Meeker Street at traffic light at bottom of hill, cross bridge over Green River, and take next left on Russell Road.

DISTANCE: 26 miles.
TERRAIN: Flat with a few minor hills.
TOTAL CUMULATIVE ELEVATION GAIN: 300 feet.
RECOMMENDED TIME OF YEAR: Any season.
RECOMMENDED STARTING TIME: Anytime.
ALLOW: 4 hours.
POINTS OF INTEREST
Trails along Green River
Interurban Trail

ELEVATION PROFILE

A handsome document published by King County in 1978 outlines the master plan for the Interurban Park Trail. Although most of the trail has been paved, only a few of the planned facilities have been constructed. When completed, this trail will provide recreational opportunities for bicyclists, joggers, hikers, and horseback riders over a distance of approximately 14.5 miles through the Green River and Stuck River valleys between Fort Dent Park in Tukwila and a trailhead in Pacific, the southern terminus. Puget Sound Power and Light Company, in a generous bid for good public relations, granted an easement over the old electric-railroad bed on which the trail is and will be built. The original electric railway between Seattle and Tacoma, dating back to the turn of the century, was a financial success for about 20 years, but as hard-surfaced, parallel roads were constructed and the era of the automobile began, decreased patronage on the electric railway eventually pulled the switch. The cities of Tukwila, Renton, Kent, Auburn, Algona, and Pacific, along with King County, are responsible for constructing and maintaining trail sections under their jurisdictions. Maintenance, including trailside mowing, sweeping, and pavement repairs, has been exemplary.

This Kent-Pacific tour follows a signed Kent bikeway to the Interurban Trail, which bypasses downtown Kent and Auburn to Algona and Pacific, where low-traffic roads continue back through Auburn. Rest rooms and picnic facilities are found in Pacific's city park, where views along the dikes of the Stuck River change with the seasons. Red-breasted merganser and goldeneye ducks make their way up the rivers during winter, while mallards and coots paddle around all year. Wintertime fishermen build small, smoky fires among the blackberry brambles along the riverbanks. Great blue herons fly regular sorties over the valley and peruse the few marshy wetlands that still remain. Many residents take advantage of the King County

North Green River Pea Patch along the Green River Road north of Auburn to grow lush vegetables in the fertile valley soil. Only a short score of years ago farming was the principal activity in the Green River Valley, but today few farmers remain. Extensive housing projects have taken the place of many of the farms, promoting the construction of new trails along the Green River and increasing the scenic byways available to bicyclists.

Combining this ride with Tour 3 from *Bicycling the Backroads Around Puget Sound* provides a scenic 40-mile backroad loop through the Green River Valley from Tukwila to Pacific.

MILEAGE LOG

0.0 City of Kent's Russell Road Park. Head north through the parking lot and bear right at Park Exit sign.

0.3 Turn right on **W. James Street** and continue on designated bikeway. Cross Washington Avenue at mile 0.9 as bikeway ends.

1.2 Turn right on **Interurban Trail** just before James Street crosses railroad tracks. Enormous metal pylons supporting high-tension power transmission lines loom overhead. The trail swings right along Willis Street at mile 1.7.

1.8 Cross Willis Street with pedestrian signal, swing left with blacktopped trail, and continue right on Interurban Trail. Cross the Green River on concrete-decked, steel-truss trail bridge at mile 2.4. Cross 277 Street at mile 3.6. Cross thoroughfares at miles 4.1, 4.5, 6.8, and 7.7. Benches under 15 Street N.W. overpass at 5.8. Bakery/deli, grocery, and cafe in Algona at 9.0; fast-food franchises one block right at 9.5.

10.1 Turn left on **3rd Avenue S.W.** in Pacific as Interurban Trail ends. Pass grocery and Pacific City Hall.

11.1 Turn right into Pacific Park. Playground equipment, picnic areas, rest rooms, river frontage along the Stuck River. Continue on **3rd Avenue S.E.** after leaving the park. Road bends left at mile 11.5 and is renamed **Skinner Road**.

SCALE OF MILES

12.0 Turn right at traffic light on **Ellingson Road**, go under railroad trestle, and turn left from left-turn lane to **A Street S.E.** Heavy traffic, but sidewalk is available.

12.3 Turn right on **37 Street S.E.**

13.0 Turn left on **M Street S.E.** Cross State Route 164 (Auburn Way S.) and continue on M Street S.E. at mile 14.2.

15.0 Turn right on **3rd Street S.E.**

15.3 Turn left on **R Street S.E.** as 3rd Street ends. Cross Main Street at mile 15.7.

16.0 Turn right on **8 Street N.E.** as R Street ends, and cross Green River. Ramped bridge sidewalk available. Road name changes to **S.E. 320 Street**.

16.2 Turn left from left-turn lane on **104 Avenue S.E.**

17.0 Turn left on **S.E. 307 Place** toward **Green River Road**. Isaac Evans Park, City of Auburn, on the left at mile 17.4; 0.4 mile of paved dike trail along the Green River with return to Green River Road. Golf course on the right at 18.0; cafe. Pea Patch gardens on the right at mile 20.0.

20.4 Bear left at stop sign as 94 Place S. comes in from the right.

20.5 Turn left through bollards on **Green River Corridor Park Trail** (City of Kent) and continue under Central Avenue bridge. Trail bends right along railroad tracks at mile 21.9.

22.0 Turn left on **S. 266 Street** as trail ends. Go under railroad trestle. Road zigzags and is renamed **79 Avenue S.**, **S. 261 Street**, and **80 Avenue S.** in quick succession.

22.6 Turn left at stop sign on **S. 259 Street**.

23.0 Go under railroad trestle, turn left on **Interurban Trail**, then immediately right on unmarked blacktopped path. Continue under State Route 167 bridge, through bollards, and onto paved roadway.

23.7 Turn left on unmarked, blacktopped path and go under Washington Street bridge. Get on paved roadway on other side as trail improvement ends. Continue through housing project on **S. 251st Street**.

24.2 Turn right at traffic circle by clock tower on **62nd Avenue S.** Go under State Route 516 bridge and by footbridge across Green River.

24.7 Bear left from roadway onto unpaved dike trail along Green River as roadway bends right on S. 249th Street. Trail pavement begins at mile 24.9. Continue past golf course. Go under Meeker Street bridge at mile 25.4.

26.3 Turn sharp right on **Russell Road** as trail ends.

26.5 Turn left into Russell Road Park; end of tour.

97   MAPLE VALLEY–VEAZIE

STARTING POINT: Lake Wilderness King County Park. From I-405 in Renton take exit 4A, Renton – Maple Valley Road S.E. (State Route 169). Drive 16 miles to Maple Valley. Turn right on Witte Road for 0.8 mile, then left into Lake Wilderness Park.

DISTANCE: 33 miles.
TERRAIN: Flat to moderate plus one steep hill.
TOTAL CUMULATIVE ELEVATION GAIN: 1500 feet.
RECOMMENDED TIME OF YEAR: All seasons.
RECOMMENDED STARTING TIME: 8 to 9 A.M.
ALLOW: 4 to 5 hours.
POINTS OF INTEREST
Maple Valley Grange
Black Diamond Bakery
Green River Gorge
Nolte State Park

ELEVATION PROFILE

In Maple Valley, near the starting point of this ride at Lake Wilderness Park, the Maple Valley Grange offers a pancake breakfast on the third Sunday of each month from 8 A.M. to 1 P.M., a great send-off for this tour. At Lake Wilderness Park a full range of facilities is offered among tall trees and green lawns. Several varieties of ducks frequent the lake, including the usual hungry, panhandling mallards. Near the park the route crosses a bridge over an abandoned railroad grade that was once used for transporting coal from the mines in and around Black Diamond.

Nolte State Park on Deep Lake is the logical picnic lunch stop for this ride. Deep Lake, the recipient of the waters of Deep Creek, has no surface outlet, but year-round springs on the edge of nearby Green River Gorge provide the obvious answer to the question of where the water goes. On opening day of fishing season, in April, the Cumberland fire hall holds a ham, eggs, and pancake breakfast.

Two other parklike facilities lie adjacent to the route: the Lake Wilderness Arboretum is at present undeveloped but has nature trails and a few picnic tables; the Green River Gorge Camp and Picnic Area, managed by the Washington State Department of Natural Resources (DNR), is primitive but creates an opportunity to incorporate this trip in an overnight tour.

Scenery on this ride is rural, with minor samples of fringe suburbia and a few short exposures to the traffic on State Route 169. Tall trees, dense forest, and bucolic cow pastures are the order of the day, with automobile traffic at a minimum. Take this tour for a different facet of versatile King County.

MILEAGE LOG

0.0   Parking lot of Lake Wilderness County Park. Leave park and head out entrance to Witte Road.

0.7   Turn left on **Witte Road S.E.** Cross Kent-Kangley Road (State Route 516) at 2.3. Witte Road eventually bends right and becomes **S.E. 276 Street**.

3.0   Turn left on **216 Avenue S.E.** as Witte Road ends. Cross railroad tracks at mile 3.4, dip down to creek valley, and climb out again. Food services available at Lake Sawyer at mile 3.9. Road bends right at mile 4.5 and is renamed **224 Avenue S.E.** Optional side trip left on S.E. 296 Street to Lake Sawyer public boat ramp with small parking area and rest rooms. At 5.7 the road changes name again to **Lake Sawyer Road S.E.**

6.6   Turn left on **S.E. Auburn–Black Diamond Road** as Lake Sawyer Road ends.

6.9   Turn right on unmarked road by small restaurant. Mailboxes indicate this is **Morgan Street**. As it enters Black Diamond, the road is renamed **Railroad Avenue**. High-calorie treats at Black Diamond Bakery at mile 7.8; doughnuts generally gone by 10:30 A.M. Continue out of town on Railroad Avenue.

8.1   Turn right on **Third Avenue (State Route 169)** and continue through dip past Jones Lake.

8.5   Turn right on **Plass Road** (unpaved) as S.R. 169 heads uphill. Follow Plass Road around a bend and uphill through forest planting, where it is named **257 Avenue S.E.** Patchy, oiled surface begins at 9.3.

9.5   Turn left on **S.E. Green Valley Road**. *Note: For connections with other tours, turn right to Flaming Geyser Park, Green River Valley, and Auburn.*

10.0   Turn right toward Enumclaw on **Enumclaw–Black Diamond Road (State Route 169)** and continue on paved 18-inch shoulder. Plunge downhill and cross Green River Gorge at 10.9. Bridge has sidewalk, allowing bicycles to stop and get off roadway for sightseeing. An eight-foot-wide paved shoulder begins on the other side of the bridge, heading uphill. Pass entrance to Green River Gorge Camp and Picnic Area (DNR) at 11.5.

12.4   Turn left on **S.E. 385 Street** as S.E. 383 Street goes right, then turn left on **Enumclaw-Franklin Road S.E.**

12.6   Turn right on **S.E. 384 Street**. After climbing a short but very steep hill, the road turns right and is renamed **276 Avenue S.E.**

13.7   Turn left on **S.E. 392 Street** as 276 Avenue ends. Continue over low ridge and descend into Enumclaw valley.

14.7   Turn left on **Veazie-Cumberland Road S.E.** toward Kanaskat and Cumberland. This open pasture area was once the community of Veazie. Cross Coal Creek at 15.0. Nolte State Park Recreation Area, suggested lunch stop, on the left at 16.2; day use only. Pass Cumberland grocery at mile 17.5 and continue on **Cumberland-Kanaskat Road S.E.** Pass Palmer-Kanaskat State Park entrance at mile 20.4, cross the Green River, and continue through Kanaskat.

21.9 Cross the main-line Burlington Northern Railroad tracks on a high bridge and turn left toward Kent on **S.E. Retreat-Kanaskat Road**. The BPA Raver power substation and high-tension switchyard is on the left as power lines pass overhead. Lake Retreat Baptist Camp is on the right.

25.3 Turn left on **Kent-Kangley Road S.E.** as Retreat Road ends.

26.4 Turn right on **Landsburg Road S.E.** toward Issaquah and North Bend by the Ravensdale Market. Crank over a hill.

27.8 Turn left on **S.E. Summit-Landsburg Road** from a downhill run.

28.6 Bear right on **S.E. 252 Street**, which shortly bends and becomes **S.E. 248 Street**. Road plays leapfrog with the Seattle Cedar River water pipeline, changing name to **240 Avenue S.E.** and eventually merging with the gravel-surfaced pipeline road for 0.1 mile.

30.4 Left turn on oiled surface of **S.E. 244 Street** by locked gate.

30.9 Turn right on **Maple Valley–Black Diamond Road S.E. (State Route 169)** and proceed along shoulder.

31.7 Turn left on **Witte Road** at traffic light.

32.5 Turn left toward Lake Wilderness County Park.

33.2 Back at starting point.

"We always get a good turnout for a food ride."

98 ENUMCLAW–AUBURN (White River)

STARTING POINT: King County Park in Enumclaw. From the north take exit 4A (State Route 169) from I-405 to Enumclaw and State Route 410 to the park. From the south take exit 135 (State Route 410) from I-5 to the park.

ALTERNATIVE STARTING POINT: Public fishing access on Green River, 2 miles east of Auburn. Take Green Valley–Black Diamond exit from State Route 18 east of Auburn, turn east on Auburn–Black Diamond Road, then right on Green Valley Road 0.1 mile to fishing access. *Note: Conservation license required.*

DISTANCE: 43 miles.
TERRAIN: Moderate with one steep hill.
TOTAL CUMULATIVE ELEVATION GAIN: 1000 feet.
RECOMMENDED TIME OF YEAR: Any season.
RECOMMENDED STARTING TIME: 9 A.M.
ALLOW: 5 hours.
POINTS OF INTEREST
Lake Tapps Pierce County Park
Auburn's Game Farm Park

ELEVATION PROFILE

The White River, as it descends from the Mud Mountain Dam near Enumclaw to the flood plain at Auburn, cuts a narrow gorge through a broad, 600- to 700-foot plateau, with Enumclaw on one side and Lake Tapps on the other. Pierce County claims the Lake Tapps plateau on the south side of the White River, while King County is the governmental entity to the north.

This tour traverses the plateau on both sides of the river, dropping briefly to the Auburn plain to recross the White River and climb out of the Green River Valley to the plateau again. These uplands as a rule remain in a semirural state with many acres devoted to pastureland for the numerous dairy farms. Horses canter along the fences in corrals and pastures by large homes scattered across the plateau. White-faced Hereford cattle graze many acres, while a carefully manicured sod farm sits near the edge of the plateau high above the White River.

The Lake Tapps power canal and aqueduct are filled by water diverted from the White River a short distance upstream from the highway bridge near Buckley. As the tour leaves Buckley, the water courses alongside through a series of lakes and canals. The aqueduct is a buried pipeline as it passes under the Sumner–Buckley Highway at the Lake Tapps Highway junction.

The tour route through Auburn avoids the heavy traffic of Auburn Way, using sidewalks and an underpass. The exposure to secondary thoroughfares, limited to a portion of Auburn's signed bicycle route, is minimal and quickly left behind. The pleasant scenery and easy terrain (with the exception of one hill) make this an enjoyable ride in southern King County.

MILEAGE LOG

0.0 Parking area of Enumclaw King County Park. Leave park and head west on **State Route 410 (Roosevelt Avenue E.)**. Keep on left-hand shoulder.

0.1 Turn left on **284 Avenue S.E.**

2.7 Turn right on **S.E. Mud Mountain Road**. White River rolls by in canyon on the left; dairy farms on the right.

5.8 Turn left on **State Route 410**. Cross the White River and enter Pierce County. Cross Lake Tapps power canal, climb hill, and enter Buckley. Cafes, groceries. Traffic busy.

6.7 Turn right on **Park Avenue** in Buckley. Road bends left and is named **Naches Street N.** at 7.1.

7.3 Turn right on **Mason Avenue**. Turn right at stop sign and cross power canal at 8.8 as road is renamed **Sumner Buckley Highway E.**

11.1 Turn right on **Buckley Tapps Highway E.** just before highway crosses power aqueduct. Continue along cliff above White River. Terrain changes from flat to rolling; traffic almost nonexistent. Pass several dairy farms. Lake Tapps comes into view at mile 15.7.

17.4 Turn left on **198 Avenue E.** toward Lake Tapps Pierce County Park.

17.8 Proceed through park gate and bear right toward peninsula park area. Rest rooms, food concession, marina, and picnic area; fair-weather lunch stop. After lunch continue north past barricade and along lakeshore dike.

18.7 Bear left on dirt path as road is barricaded ahead, then turn right on **9 Street E.**

18.8 Turn left and head downhill on **Coby Road**. Enter King County at mile 19.3. Road changes name to **Randall Avenue S.E.** and **53rd Street S.E.** as it swings left and continues downhill.

20.3 Bear right on **Kersey Way** and continue downhill. Cross the White River and continue into the city of Auburn on **R Street S.E.** Auburn's Game Farm Park, an attractive new facility with green lawns, rest rooms, and recreational facilities, appears on the right at mile 21.8. State Route 164 (Auburn Way) arches overhead at mile 22.7.

22.8 Road bends left and becomes **17 Street S.E.** To avoid heavy traffic at next corner, bicycles should get up on sidewalk. Bear right alongside **Auburn Way**.

23.1 Bear right with **M Street**, leave sidewalk, and pick up Auburn bicycle route signs. Cross railroad tracks just after State Route 18 roars overhead at mile 23.7.

23.8 Turn right with bike route sign on **3rd Street S.E.**

24.1 Turn right on **R Street S.E.** As the street turns left and rounds a corner it is renamed **Auburn–Black Diamond Road**. Execute another crossing of railroad tracks. State Route 18 crosses overhead at mile 25.5.

25.6 Turn right on **S.E. Green Valley Road**. Alternative starting point at Green River fishing access is on the left at 25.7. Strawberry fields offer U-pick opportunities during June and July.

26.6 Turn right on **Academy Drive S.E.** by a dairy farm milking Holstein-

Friesian cows. Climb a forested, winding road to the Enumclaw plateau. Seventh-Day Adventist Auburn Academy spreads over the terrain at the top of the hill at mile 27.5. Keep left with Academy Drive as it bends and twists through an attractive residential community.

27.7 Turn left on **32nd Street S.E.** at stop sign as Academy Drive ends.

28.0 Turn left on **37th Street S.E.** as busy highway appears ahead.

28.1 Continue on **Lemon Tree Lane** as 37th Street turns right.

28.5 Turn right on **Orchard Street S.E.** as Lemon Tree Lane is marked Dead End. Road is renamed **148 Avenue S.E.**

29.0 Turn left on **S.E. 368 Place** as 148 Avenue ends. Road turns left and is renamed **S.E. 372 Street**, then bends right and becomes **156 Avenue S.E.** As road bends left again, it is renamed **S.E. 376 Street**. Pass large homes on multiacre lots.

30.1 Turn right on **160 Place S.E.** Continue as S.E. 380 Place comes in from the right at stop sign at mile 30.3.

30.7 Road turns left and is renamed **S.E. 384 Street**. Mt. Rainier appears on the horizon.

31.6 Turn right on **180 Avenue S.E.** by Welcome Grange Hall. S.E. 408 Street, an old concrete highway, joins from the right at mile 33.1.

33.6 Bear left at wye with old highway as it is renamed **S.E. 416 Street**.

34.4 Bear right with old highway on **192 Place S.E.**

34.8 Bear right on old highway as it becomes **196 Avenue S.E.** Cross State Route 164 at mile 35.6. Road turns left at 36.8 and is renamed **S.E. 456 Street**. A sod farm presents acres of beautiful green lawn. *Note: If ride started from Auburn or Buckley, turn right on 220 Avenue S.E. by old schoolhouse at mile 38.4 to shorten tour by seven miles; otherwise, continue on S.E. 456 Way.*

39.1 Turn right on **S.E. 452 Street** just after 456 Street bends left (north) and is renamed **228 Avenue S.E.**

40.1 Jog left on **244 Avenue S.E.** at stop sign, then immediately turn right on **S.E. 456 Street**. Cross State Route 410 at mile 40.9. As it traverses a section of Enumclaw the road is locally renamed **Warner Avenue**.

42.6 Turn left on **284 Avenue S.E.** as S.E. 456 Street ends.

43.1 Turn right on **Roosevelt Avenue E. (State Route 410)**.

43.2 Back to starting point at Enumclaw King County Park.

PIERCE COUNTY

99   PACIFIC–LAKE TAPPS

STARTING POINT: Pacific Park, city of Pacific. From the north take exit 2A from I-405 and follow State Route 167 south to Pacific. The park is on 3rd Avenue S.E. along the Stuck River. From the south take exit 127 (State Route 512) from I-5. Pick up State Route 167 near Sumner and proceed north to Pacific.

DISTANCE: 30 miles.
TERRAIN: Hilly.
TOTAL CUMULATIVE ELEVATION GAIN: 900 feet.
RECOMMENDED TIME OF YEAR: All seasons.
RECOMMENDED STARTING TIME: 9 A.M.
ALLOW: 4 to 5 hours.
POINTS OF INTEREST
Lake Tapps Pierce County Park
Bulb farms along Puyallup River

Before the turn of the century the White River flowed north through what is now south Auburn to empty into the Green River. In one of its major rampaging floods, it overflowed the valley floor and washed a deep channel around the bluff into Stuck Creek and thence to the Puyallup River. Once settled into its new channel, it never returned to the Green. As it winds around the bluff and flows south to the Puyallup, the river is now alternatively called the White River or the Stuck River.

About 1900, the power company of Stone and Webster built a small diversion dam on the White River near the town of Buckley. A channel and flume system directed the water into a lake we know today as Lake Tapps. To make the large lake, the forest around several small lakes was logged off and gaps in the ridges diked; the stumps were left and still are visible at low water.

At the northwest corner of the lake the water follows an exit channel and plunges through penstocks to generators at the White River Power Plant, 500 feet below in the valley at Dieringer. In the early 1900s, Puget Sound Power and Light Company acquired this rather unusual system to help power its electric railways in and around Tacoma. It is still an important element in Washington State's network of electric generating facilities.

The White River originates at the terminus of the Emmons Glacier on the north slope of Mt. Rainier. After the slowly moving glacier grinds and pulverizes the rocks and soil, the silt emerges with the water at the river's source. When water is diverted from the river into the series of small lakes forming the channel to Lake Tapps, the silt settles out, forming fine, gray mud. A large dredge periodically maintains the settling basin by scooping out the mud and building up the adjoining banks.

31

About 1957, Puget Power sold land adjoining the lake to developers, retaining title of the lakefront up to the high-water, 545-foot elevation level. Since then Lake Tapps has seen the growth of an extensive residential community along its many miles of shoreline.

In winter, when river flow declines and power demand increases, Puget Power draws the lake down to feed the power turbines, slowly shrinking the reservoir and exposing huge stumps along the muddy edges. When the spring runoff begins, usually around the first of April, the company increases the diversion of water from the White River to a maximum allotment of 2000 cubic feet per second. By the middle of May, Lake Tapps is filled and ready for summer recreational activities such as powerboating, water-skiing, swimming, and bicycle touring.

Two parks offer picnicking facilities: Bonney Lake Park on the southwest corner of Lake Tapps and the Pierce County park at the northeast corner. The food concession at the county park is not open before Memorial Day, but there are picnic tables on the peninsula's lawn. A rapid, plunging return to the valley floor completes an exhilarating tour.

MILEAGE LOG

0.0   Pacific city park. Leave park and turn left (west) on **3rd Avenue S.E.**

0.4   Turn left on **Butte Avenue S.** Cross County Line Road and enter Pierce County at 0.9. Road changes name to **139th Avenue E.**

1.4   Turn right on **8th Street E.** as 139th Avenue ends.

1.6   Cross railroad tracks and turn left on **136th Avenue E.** Pass homes with small gardens, old orchard trees, and green fields.

Tail gunner

2.6 Turn left on **24th Street E.** as 136th Avenue ends. Cross railroad tracks at 2.7. Road bends right by sod farm and is renamed **142nd Avenue E.** Rhubarb and strawberry fields along the road.

4.6 Cross the Stuck River, enter Sumner, and immediately turn left on **Puyallup Street.**

5.0 Turn right on **Williams Avenue** as Puyallup ends.

5.2 Cross angled railroad tracks and turn right on **Wood Avenue.** Follow Wood through Sumner, crossing Main Street with traffic light in the city center at mile 5.7.

6.4 Turn left on **Gary Street** as Wood Avenue is marked Dead End.

6.5 Turn right on **Valley Avenue** as Gary ends.

6.8 Cross State Route 410 on overpass and almost immediately turn left on **74th Street E.** toward Riverside Drive E. Road makes a couple of bends and becomes **Riverside Drive E.** as bulb fields come into view on the left.

8.9 Turn left on **McCutcheon Road E.** as Riverside Drive goes on to cross the Puyallup River. Start uphill as the road winds around a bend.

9.9 Turn left on **Rhodes Lake Road E.** as McCutcheon crests a summit. Continue climbing through forest. Houses appear as the road levels out again.

11.2 Turn left on **Angeline Road E.** An attractive dairy farm with white-painted wooden fences adds interest to a lush, green valley. State Route 410 roars overhead at mile 12.8.

13.2 Bear left on **Old Buckley Highway** as Angeline ends.

13.5 Turn hard right on **Church Lake Road** just before the highway tops a summit by a small grocery.

14.5 Turn left on **West Tapps Drive E.** Bonney Lake Park is on the right at mile 15.2; rest rooms and picnic tables year-round; swimming beach in summer only.

15.7 Bear right on unmarked fork as main thoroughfare goes left. Missing street signs should say **West Tapps Highway E.** At the next intersection turn left on **195th Avenue N.E.** Road bends left and becomes **195 Place E.**

16.4 Turn right on **56 Street E.** as 195 Place ends. 56 Street soon bends left and is renamed **West Tapps Highway.** Overlake Island Drive goes right at 16.5. Jenks Park at mile 16.9 posts prominent Members Only signs as road is renamed **West Tapps Drive E.**

17.3 Turn right on **Lk Ridge Drive,** soon renamed **Lakeridge Drive,** and finally **176th Avenue E.** Glimpses of Lake Tapps between the houses.

18.9 Turn right on **West Tapps Drive E.** High-tension power transmission lines sizzle overhead.

19.6 Turn right on **Sumner-Tapps Highway** at stop sign. Cross power canal to penstock head gates at mile 20.5 and climb a short hill. Road is renamed successively **16th Street E.** and **182nd Avenue E.**

21.6 Turn right on **9 Street E.** as 182nd Avenue E. continues toward Auburn.

22.4 Turn right on overgrown, narrow trail behind barricade across road from grocery and cafe. The trail becomes a road along the top of a dike holding back the waters of the lake. At mile 23.1 a chain link fence and gate form another barrier on the dike road at the boundary of Lake Tapps Pierce County Park, but bicycles and pedestrians can circumvent the obstacle. The park offers picnic tables, rest rooms, and views of the lake and Mt. Rainier. A section of the park farther south along the lake offers more picnic tables, a shelter, all-season toilets, and a badminton court.

23.3 Exit the park and turn left toward park exit gate. Road becomes **198th Avenue E.** as it leaves the park.

23.7 Cross 9 Street E. and continue on **OFarrell Road E.**

24.2 Turn left on **Edwards Road E.** as OFarrell ends.

24.5 Turn right on **190th Avenue E.** as Edwards ends. Auburn city-limit sign at mile 24.7 marks the King County line. Road changes name to **Randall Avenue S.E.**

25.0 Road bends left and becomes **53rd Street S.E.**

25.7 Turn right on **Kersey Way** as 53rd Street ends. Plunge downhill as traffic picks up.

26.8 Turn left on **Oravetz Road** near bottom of hill as bridge over Stuck River comes into view.

28.2 As Oravetz ends, turn right on unmarked highway (later marked **A Street S.E.**). Almost immediately cross Stuck River on narrow, two-lane bridge with busy traffic and no sidewalks.

28.7 Turn left on **41st Street S.E.** at traffic light. Road is almost immediately renamed **Ellingson Road**. Go under railroad trestle.

28.8 Turn left on **C Street S.W.** Next street sign names it **Skinner Road**. Road turns a corner at 29.2 and becomes **3rd Avenue S.E.** as Stuck River rolls out from under railroad bridge on the left.

29.5 End of tour at Pacific Park.

100 SUMNER–LAKE TAPPS

STARTING POINT: Pierce County River Valley BMX Park in Sumner, 7800 Riverside Drive. Take the Valley Avenue exit from State Route 410 in Sumner and turn south on Valley Avenue. Turn left almost immediately on 74 Street E. toward Riverside Drive. Follow Riverside Drive 1 mile to park. Access routes to State Route 410 include the following: from the south, exit 127 from I-5 (State Route 512); from the north, exit 2A from I-405 (State Route 167).

DISTANCE: 23 miles.
TERRAIN: Rolling terrain with one major hill.
TOTAL CUMULATIVE ELEVATION GAIN: 850 feet.
RECOMMENDED TIME OF YEAR: All seasons.
RECOMMENDED STARTING TIME: 8 to 12 A.M.
ALLOW: 3 to 4 hours.
POINT OF INTEREST
Lake Tapps Pierce County Park

ELEVATION PROFILE

Water and power: these two ingredients go together in many ways, and touring around the Lake Tapps power reservoir can bring them into focus (see Tour 99). River Valley BMX Park occasionally feels their full effect when the Puyallup River reaches flood stage and deposits fine glacial silt all over the grounds of the park. Sometimes the flood waters rise high enough to cover McCutcheon Road with a thin, silty layer. Debris of twigs, pieces of wood, and vegetation lodge against the fences and among the trees and bushes, and several houses show a brown high-water mark. But nature is not always destructive; she can also be beautiful, as in the tumbling, misty, roaring spectacle of nearby Victor Falls.

Muscle power comes into play as the bicyclist negotiates steep hills up to the Lake Tapps plateau, and a plentiful supply of water is needed for the body to accomplish this feat on a hot summer day. The densely, forested hillsides and lush, green pastures project a lovely scene typical of the Northwest, the result of its surfeit of water in the form of rain.

Over much of its route this tour takes the bicyclist through forest, farmland, and inland residential areas. Occasional glimpses of Lake Tapps appear as its many arms seek avenues of escape. Mt. Rainier soars skyward from its pedestal on the southeastern end of the lake. For the adventuresome, several side roads to islands in the lake offer additional waterscape and miles of interesting exploration.

MILEAGE LOG

0.0 Parking area, Pierce County River Valley BMX Park. Leave park and turn right (south) on **Riverside Drive E.**

1.2 Turn left on **McCutcheon Road E.** as Riverside Drive bends right and approaches a bridge over the Puyallup River. Start up steep hill at mile 1.9.

2.2 Turn left on **Rhodes Lake Road** at summit of hill and continue climbing for another 0.8 mile.

3.5 Turn left on **Angeline Road E.** State Route 410 roars overhead at mile 5.1.

5.6 Continue on **Old Buckley Highway E.** as it enters from the right and go uphill on old concrete pavement.

5.9 Turn sharp right on **Church Lake Road** as Old Buckley Highway approaches a summit by a grocery store.

7.5 Continue on **Kelly Lake Road E.** as it enters from the right at a small wye.

7.9 Turn left on **214 Ave E.** as Kelly Lake Road ends.

8.2 Turn right on **Connells Prairie Road E.**

9.1 Bear left on **Barkubein Road E.** by Connells Prairie Battle Monument. Cross bridge over Lake Tapps power flume at 9.2. As it bends right at mile 9.9, the road is renamed **Radke Road East**.

10.2 Turn left on **Buckley Tapps Highway E. (230th Avenue E.).** As it makes several bends the road is renamed successively **40th Street E.**, **214th Avenue E.**, **210th Avenue E.**, and **12th Street E.** *Note: An interesting optional side trip is presented on the left at mile 12.8 on Island Park Way. Several miles of marked-off cycle paths and unusual views of Lake Tapps.*

15.1 Turn left and uphill on **198 Avenue E.** toward Lake Tapps Pierce County Park.

15.4 Proceed through park gate and bear right toward peninsula park area. Rest rooms, concessions, and picnic area; fair-weather lunch stop. After lunch continue north past barricade and along lakeshore dike road.

16.5 Bear left on dirt path as road is barricaded ahead, then walk bicycles down embankment and turn left on **9 Street E.** Grocery and cafe at this turn.

17.0 Turn left on **182nd Avenue E.** The road winds up and down and crosses the power canal to the White River Power Plant penstocks at 18.2.

19.1 Go straight on **Sumner-Tapps Highway E.** as West Tapps Highway goes left. Climb a short rise and enjoy a long, straight descent.

21.4 Pass under State Route 410 and continue on **166 Avenue E. (Wahle Road E.).**

22.3 Turn right on **78th Street E. (Wood McCumber Road E.)** as 166th Avenue ends.

22.5 Turn left on **Riverside Drive E.**, then right into entrance of River Valley BMX Park to end the ride.

101   BUCKLEY–ORTING

STARTING POINT: White River High School Annex in Buckley. From the south, take exit 127 (State Route 512) from I-5 to the State Route 410 interchange and take State Route 410 east to Buckley. From the north, take exit 2A from I-405 and follow State Route 167 and State Route 410 to Buckley. Turn east on A Street as Park Avenue goes west at the northeast edge of town and park along A Street by high school annex.

ALTERNATIVE STARTING POINT: Lions Club Park in Orting. Take Valley Avenue exit from State Route 410 in Sumner and follow State Route 162 south to Orting.

DISTANCE: 32 miles.
TERRAIN: Hilly with some flat.
TOTAL CUMULATIVE ELEVATION GAIN: 800 feet.
RECOMMENDED TIME OF YEAR: All seasons.
RECOMMENDED STARTING TIME: 9 A.M.
ALLOW: 5 hours.
POINTS OF INTEREST
Victor Falls
Puyallup Salmon Hatchery

ELEVATION PROFILE

Located in northeastern Pierce County, Buckley and Orting trace their origins back to the 1870s and 1880s, when settlers of European extraction arrived to farm and log the land, work for the Northern Pacific Railroad, or dig coal in the nearby mining towns of Wilkeson, Carbonado, and Burnett.

Today, a century later, logging continues to be an important industry in the nearby Cascade foothills, but the mining operations stopped many years ago. The Northern Pacific moved its main line north to Kanaskat in King County, merging in 1970 with the Chicago, Burlington and Quincy to form the Burlington Northern Railroad. Farming, also, is no longer important to the economy of Buckley, and only a few dairy farms persist near Orting. Pierce County is slowly but surely losing its agricultural lands, yet it still maintains a rural atmosphere.

As this bicycle tour leaves Buckley, it passes small, private woodlots and homes with orchards, gardens, horses, cows, sheep, and chickens. Hinkle-man Road, narrow and patchy, is not conducive to fast-moving traffic. Pleasant country scenery continues along 112 Street E. (formerly called Pipeline Road), which follows the Tacoma water pipeline originating high up the Green River Gorge. The view from the ridge overlooking the sparsely settled South Prairie Creek Valley 300 feet below is most impressive. Winter tourists may catch a glimpse of ducks on little Rhodes Lake as they round a corner and begin the exhilarating plunge downhill to the Puyallup River Valley. Several small streams tumble off the hillside and rush noisily to the silt-laden Puyallup. At McMillin, traffic picks up along State Route 162, but a

39

frontage road beside a former bulb farm, now platted for residential development, lessens the ordeal of this section of highway. Massive Mt. Rainier appears in all its glory at the end of the valley, brightening the spirits of all.

State Route 162 has three-foot-wide paved shoulders as it leaves Orting and heads up the valley of South Prairie Creek, which joins the Carbon, another silt-laden river, near the traffic-free backroad of Pioneer Way. Horses occupy the small pastures near the homes along the Lower Burnett Road. Old masonry structures, possibly once powder magazines for the coal mines, crumble among the trees. The route continues along this narrow, winding road as it negotiates the steep, enchanting canyon of South Prairie Creek and emerges on top of the plateau at the old mining town of Burnett, where rows of look-alike "company" houses line the street. Traffic continues to be minimal and scenery rural as the route returns to Buckley.

MILEAGE LOG

0.0 White River High School Annex in Buckley. Head west on **North A Street**, cross Highway 410, and continue on **Park Avenue**. Road bends left at mile 0.6 and is renamed **Naches Street N.**

0.8 Turn right on **Mason Avenue** at stop sign.

1.0 Bear left, then right on **Hinkleman Road E.** at unmarked wye and proceed along narrow, oiled roadway.

1.9 Turn left on **Mundy Loss Road E.** at stop sign as Hinkleman ends. Cross State Route 410 at mile 2.0.

2.3 Turn right on **112th Street E.** A small airstrip appears on the left at mile 4.0.

5.9 Turn sharp left on **South Prairie Road E.**

6.3 Turn right on **Prairie Ridge Drive E.**

6.5 Turn right on **120th Street E.** as Prairie Ridge Drive continues into the mobile-home community of Prairie Ridge.

8.1 Turn right on **198th Avenue E.** as 120th Street ends. The marshy shores of Rhodes Lake show dimly through the trees on the left. The road bends left at 8.4 and is renamed **Rhodes Lake Road E.** A tall surge pipe for the Tacoma water line stands on the left. At mile 9.4, near the bottom of a downhill run, the water department facilities of Bonney Lake appear on the left. Just beyond the end of the fence and guardrail, a faint trail leads 30 yards or so to the precipice of Victor Falls. Caution is urged in exploring here; there are no guardrails, and a slip may result in a vertical fall of 70 feet. Victor Falls is the property of Bonney Lake, and authorized tours may be arranged by calling city hall at (206) 863-6318.

10.9 Bear left at wye on **McCutcheon Road E.** View of Puyallup River below.

12.2 Bear right on **128th Street E.** and cross the Puyallup River as road ahead is marked Dead End. The Tacoma Water Department pipeline crosses its own bridge on the left.

12.9 Turn left on **State Route 162** by McMillin Grocery.

14.4 Turn right on **Old Pioneer Way E.** and continue parallel to highway.

15.9 Continue right on **State Route 162** as Old Pioneer Way ends. Orting Lions Club Park on the right in Orting at 16.7; picnic lunch stop. A drive-in before the park and a cafe beyond offer indoor lunches. Follow S.R. 162 through Orting as it bends right and left.

18.1 Bear left with S.R. 162 as Orville Road E. goes right to Electron. Puyallup Salmon Hatchery on the left at 19.2.

20.4 Turn right on **South Pioneer Way** and continue parallel to the highway.

24.8 Turn left in South Prairie on **Emory Avenue** as Pioneer Way ends, then turn right on **State Route 162** and pass a grocery store on the left. Climb hill out of town.

25.9 Turn right and down a short hill on **Lower Burnett Road**. Road meanders along South Prairie Creek with Mt. Rainier in the distance. Cross bridge over creek at 27.2 and start uphill.

27.6 Turn left on **State Route 165** in old mining town of Burnett. Cross high bridge over South Prairie Creek.

28.4 Bear left at wye on **State Route 162** toward South Prairie and Orting.

28.6 Cross bridge over abandoned railroad cut and turn right on **Mundy Loss Road E.** toward White River Middle School.

29.6 Turn right on **112th Street E.**

30.8 Turn right at wye on **State Route 165**, then immediately left on **River Avenue**. Roadside park with picnic tables on the left. Continue on River Avenue through Buckley.

31.5 Turn right on **A Street** at stop sign and return to starting point.

102 GRAHAM–NORTHWEST TREK

STARTING POINT: Parking lot of Graham Grange Hall in Graham. From the north take exit 2A from I-405 and follow State Route 167, State Route 512, and State Route 161 (south) to Graham. From the south take exit 127 (State Route 512) from I-5 and State Route 161 south to Graham. Park near the grange hall across from the Graham Post Office on 224th Street E.

DISTANCE: 40 miles.
TERRAIN: Moderate to hilly.
TOTAL CUMULATIVE ELEVATION GAIN: 1200 feet.
RECOMMENDED TIME OF YEAR: Any season.
RECOMMENDED STARTING TIME: 9 A.M.
ALLOW: 5 to 9 hours.
POINT OF INTEREST
Northwest Trek, Tacoma's zoological park

Northwest Trek, a wildlife preserve created from a 600-acre cattle ranch, perches atop a plateau overlooking Ohop Lake near Eatonville. Originally just a dream of two private citizens, it shows what can be accomplished when diligent efforts are made to obtain the cooperation of local governmental agencies and the financial help of the general public.

Dr. and Mrs. David Hellyer had the vision of a park devoted to the exhibition and preservation of northwest animals and birds in their native habitat. They wanted the animals free to roam about their ranch, each species occupying its own ecological niche on the land. The Hellyers also wanted the public to be able to observe the animals. In 1971 they approached the Tacoma Metropolitan Park Board with an offer: they would donate the land for the natural zoo in return for the privilege of remaining in their home on the shore of Horseshoe Lake for as long as they desired. The park board approved the idea and put a bond issue before the citizens of Tacoma to fund the park. It took two tries, but in 1973 the people of Tacoma voted for the bond issue and Northwest Trek became a reality, opening its door to visitors in July 1975. A major portion of the park is enclosed by a secure fence to exclude predators and to allow animals to roam freely. In propane-powered trams, visitors travel 5.5 miles of paved road to view the wildlife within the enclosure. Herds of bison, elk, and antelope graze the green meadows while caribou and white- and black-tailed deer browse the forest. Bighorn sheep and mountain goats climb the ridges, and moose seek out the wetlands. Wild turkey gobblers make their cacophonic proclamations and strut for the benefit of their hens. Canada geese stake out nesting areas by several small marshy lakes; one such lake boasts a beaver lodge. Ubiquitous mallards and coots prefer the big lake and are occasionally joined by rarer species such as gadwall and wood duck. Trumpeter and tundra swans add their beauty to the scene. Great blue herons fly in and out of the ponds and lakes, and sandhill cranes challenge the trams for domination of the roadways. Changing with the seasons, the wild bird population attracts the avid bird watcher.

Outside the main herbivore area, predatory large cats, timber wolves, and bears have separate fenced enclosures with natural settings. The public is invited to walk through a display area that has been cleverly designed so that small animals such as otter, beaver, raccoon, fisher, skunk, marten, and wolverine appear in a natural outdoor setting among man-made dens, lodge, stream, and ponds.

A five-mile nature trail traverses the hillside overlooking Ohop Lake and offers the hiker interesting botanical explorations. Picnic tables, food service, gift shop, and rest rooms complement this unique wildlife preserve.

While bird and wild animal lovers will enjoy Northwest Trek, those who relish the sight of wildflowers growing in their natural state will find a variety of species along the roadsides of this tour; flowers of the open prairie, dense forest, and lush greensward weave a colorful tapestry.

MILEAGE LOG

0.0 Leave grange hall parking lot, turn right on **224th Street E.**, and proceed gently downhill. Cross railroad tracks at mile 0.8. Fenced pastures with cattle.

1.9 Turn left on **70th Avenue E.** Pass a small group of homes and enter forest. Mahonia and kinnikinnick grow in the stony soil.

4.1 Turn right on **260th Street E.** Horse ranches with occasional large oak trees in the pastures alternate with forests of Douglas fir.

5.6 Jog left on **State Route 7** as 260th Street appears to end, then turn right and continue on 260th Street. In the springtime blue camas lilies and blue campanulas (bluebells) bloom along the roadside and underneath the trees in the open forest.

7.5 Bear left with 260th Street E. as Rice Kandle Road E. continues on. Meadowlarks sing from trees and wires.

8.1 Turn left on **8th Avenue E.** as 260th Street E. ends. Military Reservation is on the right. Cross two small creeks. Stop and cross 304th Street E. at mile 10.8. Road bends left at mile 12.3 and becomes **Kinsman Road E.** as forest closes in.

14.2 Turn left on **State Route 702** as Kinsman is marked Dead End. Proceed through Weyerhaeuser Tree Farm, harvested and replanted in 1963 and thinned in 1992.

16.4 Junction with State Route 7 as S.R. 702 ends. Cross S.R. 7 and continue on **Eatonville Cutoff**, which shortly bends right.

18.6 Turn left on **Jensen Road E.** as Eatonville Cutoff proceeds downhill. Road is narrow and winds through forest. Pastures open up around a small lake. Road bends left and up a very steep hill at mile 19.8.

20.6 Turn left on **State Route 161** as Jensen Christian Road ends.

20.7 Turn right on **Trek Drive E.** toward Northwest Trek.

21.8 Northwest Trek, a Pacific Northwest wildlife preserve. Open daily 9:30 A.M. until one hour before sundown, April through October. Open Wednesday through Sunday from November through March.

Children are half price; group rates for 12 or more are available on request. After visiting the park retrace route back to park entrance on **Trek Drive E.**

22.8 Turn right on **State Route 161**.

25.0 Bear left on **Benston Road E.** toward Camp Arnold at milepost 11. Road is shortly renamed **Webster Road E.**

27.5 Turn right on **Kapowsin Highway (304th Street E.)** at stop sign.

31.4 Continue with **Orville Road E.** as it joins from the right at blinking red light. Grocery at this corner.

31.8 Cross bridge over railroad tracks and immediately bear left on **Griggs Road E.** Lake Kapowsin appears below on the right.

31.9 Turn left uphill on **Browne Road E.** and zigzag right and left through Kapowsin on **296th Street E.** and **158th Avenue E.** Pedal over several short hills.

34.2 Turn left on **264th Street E.** as 158th Avenue ends. Morgan Lake appears in a pasture on the left at 34.5. Cross Orting-Kapowsin Highway E. and railroad tracks at 35.3. Magnificent view of Mt. Rainier to the east.

37.2 Turn right on **110th Avenue E.** and climb a hill past dairy farm. On a clear day in spring Mt. Rainier appears white all the way to the bottom of its 14,000-foot massif. Top the hill at 38.4 and plunge down the other side. Road zigzags left and right as it is renamed **240th Street E.** and **108th Avenue E.**

39.8 Turn left on **224th Street E.** as 108th Avenue ends. Cross State Route 161 at mile 40.2.

40.3 End of tour by Graham Grange Hall in downtown Graham.

103 GRAHAM–ROY–KAPOWSIN

STARTING POINT: Parking lot of Graham Grange Hall in Graham. From the north take exit 2A from I-405 and follow State Route 167, State Route 512, and State Route 161 (south) to Graham. From the south take exit 127 (State Route 512) from I-5 and State Route 161 south to Graham. Park near the grange hall across from the Graham Post Office on 224th Street E.

DISTANCE: 40 miles.
TERRAIN: Flat to moderate.
TOTAL CUMULATIVE ELEVATION GAIN: 1000 feet.
RECOMMENDED TIME OF YEAR: Any season.
RECOMMENDED STARTING TIME: 9 to 10 A.M.
ALLOW: 5 to 6 hours.
POINTS OF INTEREST None outstanding

ELEVATION PROFILE

Cows graze unconcernedly in broad open prairies; a few turn their heads to watch bicycles as they wheel by. Deciduous trees, bare of leaves in winter, support a crop of lichens reminiscent of biblical tales of manna. Occasional swampy patches grow crops of cattails and steeplebush. Blue camas lilies along the roadside in spring are followed in summer by bluebell campanulas and tall orange tiger lilies.

At almost the halfway point, Roy offers a cafe, grocery, delicatessen, and park picnicking facilities. An old railroad water tank has been rehabilitated as a standpipe for the town's water supply. Next door to the rodeo grounds, a colorful sign reminiscent of the early Wild West advertises an old tavern. These are the highlights of this tour; details may be filled in by the rider.

MILEAGE LOG

0.0 Leave grange hall parking lot and turn right on **224th Street E.**
1.1 Turn right on **82nd Avenue E.** Road bends left at mile 1.8 and is renamed **Eustis-Hunt Road E.**
2.5 Turn left on **204th Street E.** as Eustis-Hunt Road ends. Road executes bends to left and right and is renamed **Knoble Road E., 200th Street E.,** and **38th Avenue E.**
5.6 Turn left on **192nd Avenue E.** just after crossing railroad tracks.
7.7 Turn left on **8 Avenue E.** Cross State Route 7 at mile 8.3. Gas station and cafe.
8.8 Turn right on **208th Street E.**
9.8 Turn left on **State Route 507** and proceed along paved shoulder. Enter Roy city limits at mile 16.3. As it enters main part of town, road bends right, then left on **McNaught Street**. *Note: To visit city park, go straight on Water Street as highway bends left. Park is at foot of Water Street, accessible by footbridge over Muck Creek.*
16.6 Roy city center. Grocery and cafe; lunch stop. After lunch, head back

(north) along **State Route 507**.

16.7   Bear right on **280th Street S.** as S.R. 507 swings left. Cross railroad tracks at mile 17.1. Road turns corner at mile 18.4 and is renamed **56th Avenue S.**

18.9   Turn left on **288th Street S.** as 56th Avenue is marked Dead End.

21.0   Turn right on **24th Avenue S.**

21.4   Bear left on **Schudy Road** as 24th Avenue goes on unpaved.

22.1   Turn left on **304th Street S.** Cross State Route 7 at mile 26.9 and continue as 304th Street is renamed **Kapowsin Highway E.** Grocery. Cross State Route 161 at mile 29.7.

32.9   Turn left on **Orting-Kapowsin Highway E.** at flashing light in Kapowsin. Grocery, tavern.

37.9   Turn left on **224th Street E.** at blinking amber light. This is Thrift. Cross State Route 161 in Graham at 39.8 and return to starting point by Graham Grange Hall.

"He is really sold on the advantages of sew-ups."

104 OHOP–ROY

STARTING POINT: Public fishing access on Lake Ohop. From the Seattle area take exit 2A from I-405, and follow State Route 167, State Route 512, and State Route 161 (south) to Orville Road E. Turn left and proceed 0.5 mile to fishing access. From the south take exit 127 (State Route 512) from I-5 and State Route 161 south 20 miles to Orville Road E. Turn left and proceed 0.5 mile to fishing access. *Note: Parking privileges may require conservation license, available for a nominal fee at sporting goods stores.* Additional parking areas along road shoulder north of access.

DISTANCE: 55 miles.
TERRAIN: Moderate to hilly.
TOTAL CUMULATIVE ELEVATION GAIN: 2000 feet.
RECOMMENDED TIME OF YEAR: Any season.
RECOMMENDED STARTING TIME: 9 A.M.
ALLOW: 7 to 8 hours.
POINT OF INTEREST
Views of Mt. Rainier

ELEVATION PROFILE

DISTANCE IN MILES

Houses crowd the shoreline along Lake Ohop, allowing glimpses of the lake and recreational boaters. A spring, gushing through a pipe to a concrete basin along the road, is a popular stop for motorists and bicyclists alike. Faint smoke plumes rise from the brick kilns at Clay City near the head of Ohop Lake as the valley continues to the end of Lake Kapowsin. The tall silhouette of Mt. Rainier stands on the horizon, overlooking the upland plateaus and valleys of southern Pierce County. Poorly suited to grain or vegetable crops, the land supports a suburban fringe of houses, grass for dairy and beef cattle and riding horses, and trees from which more houses will be built.

Open prairies, some natural and some with an assist from *Homo sapiens*, green up in spring with a lush crop of grass. Prairie flowers such as the blue camas lily brighten the roadsides. Signs proclaim the border between the Fort Lewis Military Reservation and open cattle range. (Watch out for the cattle guards!) Mounds of the western thatching ant, some as tall as three feet, digest a continually refreshed crop of grasses and needles.

The trees at first seem merely decorative: open-grown firs and lichen-covered oaks. Occasional stands of fir are overcrowded, badly in need of thinning. But these are private lands, neglected by Paul Bunyan for many years. When the commercial forest (primarily Weyerhaeuser) appears, the hillsides bear evidence of the giant's fabled scythe. But all is not desolation, as young trees, hand planted and cared for, are turning the hills green again for another crop of timber several decades hence.

From the hilltops the route descends to the glacial valley of the Ohop. Eventually the creek winds back to its source at Ohop Lake and the starting point for this tour.

MILEAGE LOG

0.0 Public fishing access on Ohop Lake. Leave parking area and turn right on **Orville Road E.**

8.1 Stop at blinking red light and continue on **Orting-Kapowsin Highway E.**

8.7 Turn left on **288th Street E.** Cross State Route 161 at mile 11.5.

13.0 Turn right on **Webster Road E.** as 288th Street ends. Gain summit, descend steep hill. Road changes name to **70th Avenue E.**

14.9 Turn left on **260th Street E.**

16.3 Turn left on **State Route 7**, then immediately right again on **260th Street E.** Cross cattle guard and enter open range area at mile 17.8.

18.1 Bear left with 260th Street E. as Rice Kandle Road E. continues on.

18.8 Turn left on **8th Avenue E.** as 260th Street E. ends and cross another cattle guard. Leave range area. Cross Muck Creek and South Creek.

20.5 Turn right on **288th Street E.** just before 8th Avenue E. starts up a long, steep hill. Large ant hills appear near mile 21.7. Cross Lacamas Creek at mile 24.0.

24.5 Turn right on **56th Avenue S.** Cross Lacamas Creek. Road bends left at mile 25.0 and is renamed **280th Street S.**

26.5 Cross railroad tracks and bear left on **State Route 507** into Roy.

26.6 Continue on **Water Street** toward city park as State Route 507 turns left to business district on McNaught Street (cafe, grocery). Cross railroad tracks, jog right on **Warren Street**, and continue on **Water Street** to end, where a footbridge leads right across Muck Creek to park at mile 26.8; lunch stop. After lunch, recross footbridge and head south on **Rounge Street**.

27.0 Turn left on **Huggins-Grieg Road** by rodeo grounds.

27.2 Turn right on **McNaught Street (State Route 507)** and ride out of town.

27.6 Turn left on **288th Street S.**

28.3 Bear right on **Lyons Road S.** as 288th Street bends left. Road is renamed **74th Avenue S.**, **70th Avenue S.**, and **72nd Avenue S.** in succession.

30.4 Turn left on **Tisch Road**. High-tension power lines hum overhead one mile later. Road changes name to **56 Avenue S.**

33.0 Turn right on **State Route 702**, then left on **58th Avenue S.** After 0.5 mile the road bends right and becomes **360 Street S.**

34.7 Turn sharp left on **Harts Lake Road S.** At mile 38.7 a side road goes right to Harts Lake public fishing access with toilets.

40.0 Bend left with thoroughfare on **8th Avenue S.**

42.7 Turn right at stop sign on **State Route 702**.

46.7 Cross State Route 7 and continue on **Eatonville Cutoff** as it bears right toward Eatonville.

51.5 Turn right toward Eatonville on **State Route 161** as Eatonville Cutoff ends. Dogwood Park with view of Mt. Rainier on the left 0.2 mile later.

52.1 Turn right on **Ohop Valley Road E.**

52.3 Continue on **Ohop Valley Road Extension E.** as Ohop Valley Road turns right to Pioneer Farm Museum. Cross Ohop Creek at mile 54.1.

54.4   Turn sharp left on **State Route 161 (Eatonville Highway)**.

54.5   Go by Ski Park Road and bear right on next road, marked Dead End.
Go around barricades and cross bridge.

54.9   Turn right on **Orville Road E.** and cycle along Ohop Lake.

55.4   Turn right into fishing access on Ohop Lake; end of tour.

"Is this the Skyline Trail?"

105 MT. RAINIER

STARTING POINT: King County Fairgrounds, Enumclaw. From the south take exit 127 (State Route 512) from I-5 to Puyallup and State Route 410 to Enumclaw. From the north take exit 142A (State Route 18) from I-5 to Auburn and State Route 164 to Enumclaw, or from I-405 take exit 4A (State Route 169) to Enumclaw. Turn right from S.R. 410 by Farman's Pickle Factory on 248 Avenue S.E. as highway leaves Enumclaw, and proceed south 0.5 mile to King County Fairgrounds. Park inside gates. (Make arrangements with fairground manager.)

DISTANCE: Total, 162 miles: first day, 63 miles; second day, 43 miles; third day, 56 miles.
TERRAIN: Mountainous.
TOTAL CUMULATIVE ELEVATION GAIN: 10,100 feet: first day, 2800 feet; second day, 4200 feet; third day, 3100 feet.
RECOMMENDED TIME OF YEAR: Weekend after Labor Day to first weekend in October.
RECOMMENDED STARTING TIME: 8 to 9 A.M.
ALLOW: 3 days.
POINTS OF INTEREST
Mt. Rainier National Park
Views of Mt. Rainier

ELEVATION PROFILE FIRST DAY

ELEVATION PROFILE SECOND DAY

ELEVATION PROFILE THIRD DAY

Until a few decades ago Paradise Park on the slopes of Mt. Rainier was at the terminus of a dead-end road. With the completion of the Stevens Canyon Road in 1957, it became a short side trip on a popular weekend drive. Addition of a wide, well-graded access road, attractive visitor center, and extensive hard-surfaced walking trails makes Paradise a popular tourist center with a crowded parking lot. The popularity of the area for automotive traffic during the summer and closure of roads by snow at other times of the year, limit to a few short weeks in autumn the optimum interval for enjoying this tour by bicycle. Even then, the possibility of sudden changes of weather requires precautionary planning and provisions.

In order to protect automobiles parked at the starting point during the tour, it is recommended that arrangements be made with the King County Fairground manager (telephone (206) 825-7777) to park inside the locked gates of the fairground complex. A fee is charged for this service.

Dairy farms dominate the scene as bicyclists leave the fairgrounds and ride along the White River. The rough shoulders and busy traffic of State Route 410 are endured for a brief river crossing. Traffic is minimal through the Pierce County towns of Buckley and South Prairie as open, rural vistas greet the eye along South Prairie Creek. The route turns south along the Puyallup River, where a small lumber mill processes logs beside Orville Road. The high canyon crossing of the Puyallup River affords a view of the milky-gray waters, full of silt from the Tahoma and Puyallup glaciers on Mt. Rainier. Summer cabins and an increasing number of year-round residences line the delightful winding road along Ohop Lake.

Occasional striking views of Mt. Rainier along the Alder Cutoff Road near Eatonville give the camera buff reasons for stopping. An operating passenger steam train beckons in Elbe for a no-effort side trip to Mineral to view the mountain from a different vantage point. Foothills block the view as the Nisqually entrance to Mt. Rainier National Park is approached, but the mountain soon appears in all its glory. Blazing patches of red and yellow splash across the hillsides and stand out against the gray rock and evergreen trees. Icy-white glaciers sparkling against a bright blue sky complete the colorful autumn spectacle.

Several points along the way, such as the Kautz Mudflow, entice the cyclist to stop and enjoy the inspiring vistas or walk the short scenic trails. In 1947 torrential rains caused the snout of the Kautz glacier to collapse, damming the canyon and forming a lake. Eventually the lake broke through and surged down the creek canyon, carrying tons of rock and mud into the forest below and wiping out everything before it. In keeping with National Park Service land management policy, natural forces were left to heal the scars of this devastating flood. Today a new forest is growing in the soil brought down with the avalanche.

Spectacular Christine and Narada falls provide welcome excuses for stopping on the way up to Paradise, as do metal plaques explaining the views from Rieksecker Point and Canyon Rim. The gray (Canada) jay and Clark's nutcracker enjoy sharing a bit of your lunch at these viewpoints, and also are popular attractions at the Paradise Visitor Center. Dressed in their mid-season brown-and-white attire, white-tailed ptarmigans occasionally stop traffic as they cross the road near the Paradise summit. In winter their all-white plumage makes them practically invisible against the snow.

In season, flowers of all colors and shapes cover the gentle slopes above the Paradise Visitor Center. Hard-surfaced trails lead travelers to a fantastic alpine garden. Strict adherence to trail travel is encouraged to protect the fragile vegetation and to keep erosion of the fine pumice soil to a minimum. At an elevation of 5420 feet, the weather at Paradise can be capricious

during early fall, so bicyclists must be prepared for colder temperatures. Warm clothes should be available for the downhill trip to Ohanapecosh. As the road begins its descent of the Paradise Valley, brown furry marmots sun themselves on large boulders. Framed by red-and-gold-leafed huckleberry bushes, Reflection Lakes double the grandeur by duplicating the image of the magnificent mountain. The road then executes a sharp hairpin turn as it plunges down the canyon. Shrubby Sitka alder and vine maple cling to the steep ridge on the north side, while several waterfalls cascade down the slopes to the south. The second of two tunnels signals the approach to the box canyon of the Muddy Fork of the Cowlitz River, where rest rooms and a scenic overlook provide a welcome stopping place. Golden-mantled ground squirrels and chipmunks frequent the area, accepting handouts and surreptitiously rummaging through handlebar bags or panniers for other tasty morsels. The viewpoint by Backbone Ridge offers one last look before the road traverses the Cowlitz Divide and dives down into the narrow Ohanapecosh Valley. Just before the road crosses the Ohanapecosh River, a sign proclaims a side trip to the Grove of the Patriarchs. A one-mile trail leads past many huge old cedars and Douglas fir trees growing on an island in the river. Ohanapecosh, once a popular spa with cabins and baths that used water piped from hot springs, is now just another park campground. The cabins and baths have been removed and the hot springs restored to their original state. A spacious visitor center provides extensive displays of geology, natural history, and wildlife.

There are few views of Mt. Rainier on the road to Cayuse Pass, but the dense evergreen forest, laced with deciduous shrubs and trees, presents a beautiful scene, and in early fall the coming of winter can be presaged by snow. Again, plenty of warm clothes must be available for the descent from Cayuse Pass. Once the descent is begun, the exhilarating pace discourages bicyclists from frequent stops. One mountain viewpoint requires crossing the highway, as do views of the White River channel. The roadside waterfalls of Crystal Springs are interesting but unheralded by signs. At the base of the hill, soon after leaving national forest land, the shoulder widens, lessening competition with the fast automotive traffic. Without the scenic attractions of the mountain and its waterfalls, prevailing tailwinds encourage bicyclists to complete this tour rapidly.

MILEAGE LOG

FIRST DAY

0.0 King County Fairgrounds, Enumclaw. Leave fairgrounds and turn left (south) on **284 Avenue S.E.**

2.3 Turn right on **Mud Mountain Road**. White River rolls by on the left.

5.5 Turn left on **Enumclaw-Buckley Road (State Route 410)**. Cross the White River, climb a hill, and enter Buckley.

6.3 Turn left by drive-in on **Park Avenue**, then right on **River Avenue**.

7.1 Continue on **State Route 165** as it joins from the right.

8.6 Turn right on **State Route 162** toward South Prairie at road junction. Pass through South Prairie at mile 11.1. Cross the Carbon River at mile 15.3. Puyallup Salmon Hatchery at mile 17.0.

17.5 Turn left on **Orville Road E.** as S.R. 162 continues right into Orting. Cross Puyallup River at 21.0. Road to Electron (park, view) goes left at mile 24.5.

26.7 Turn left with Orville Road E. at Kapowsin Junction (blinking red light, grocery). Route continues south along Lake Kapowsin and Ohop Lake toward Eatonville.

35.4 Pass public fishing access and at 35.7 turn left on faint trail to a partially barricaded bridge across Ohop Creek. Cross bridge and continue on roadway on other side.

36.0 Bear left and uphill on **State Route 161**.

36.7 Turn right on business route in Eatonville by Eatonville sign. Grocery and cafes.

37.1 Turn left on **Center Street E.** by U.S. Post Office. As the road leaves town it is marked **Alder Cutoff**. A climb to two summits precedes a short descent to Alder Lake.

44.5 Turn left on **State Route 7** toward Mt. Rainier National Park. Tacoma City Light Alder Lake Recreation Area on the right at mile 47.8. Enter Elbe at mile 49.2. Cafe, grocery, steam train rides. Watch for acute-angled railroad tracks.

49.4 Continue on **State Route 706** in Elbe as S.R. 7 goes right toward Morton. Pass through Ashford at 56.9; last grocery for two days. Sign points right on Kernahan Road two miles to Big Creek National Forest Camp and Skate Creek Road at mile 59.7; overnight camping. Pass Copper Creek Inn at mile 60.8 and Alexander's Manor at 62.0.

63.4 Nisqually entrance to Mt. Rainier National Park; motel, several lodges, and bed-and-breakfast accommodations nearby. Sunshine Point Campground is another 0.3 mile past the entrance.

SECOND DAY

0.0 From the Nisqually entrance, where a nominal entrance fee is levied on bicyclists, continue into Mt. Rainier National Park. Pass Sunshine

Point Campground at mile 0.3; Kautz Mudflow at 3.3.

6.4 Park headquarters at Longmire, elevation 2761 feet; nature trail, cafeteria and snack bar; Cougar Rock Campground entrance at 8.6.

10.6 Christine Falls, elevation 3676 feet; scenic footpath to view falls from under bridge.

11.8 Cross Nisqually River; elevation 3900 feet.

12.8 Bear right to Rieksecker Point Overlook; elevation 4212 feet.

13.9 Rejoin main road. View of Mt. Rainier from Canyon Rim Overlook at mile 14.5; elevation 4462 feet.

15.6 Narada Falls on the right; rest rooms and footpath to view of falls.

16.4 Bear left toward Paradise at road junction. Begin a steep, two-mile climb ending at Paradise Visitor Center at mile 18.4; elevation 5420 feet. Cafeteria and snack bar open through first weekend in October. After exploring the many interesting exhibits, trails, and vistas, continue uphill past Paradise Inn and start downhill on one-way road.

21.0 Join main road and turn left toward Ohanapecosh. Pass Reflection Lakes at mile 22.5. Brake around a horseshoe turn at mile 24.6 and continue down **Stevens Canyon Road**. Proceed through two tunnels and emerge at Box Canyon of the Muddy Fork of the Cowlitz River at mile 29.5; rest rooms and scenic overlook. Road continues downhill for two more miles before climbing again to a summit at mile 34.3, then dropping to a crossing of the Ohanapecosh River (elevation 2176 feet) at mile 40.0.

40.1 Turn right on **State Route 123** toward Ohanapecosh.

41.9 Turn right into Ohanapecosh Campground. Visitor center at 42.2. No food concessions. Campground area begins 0.2 mile farther.

THIRD DAY

0.0 Leave Ohanapecosh Campground and turn left on **State Route 123**. Pass Stevens Canyon entrance to Mt. Rainier National Park at mile 2.3 and continue toward Cayuse Pass. Cross Panther Creek at mile 4.6 and begin inexorable climb. Pass massive rock outcroppings at mile 7.0; views into canyon below. Owyhigh Lakes Trail goes right at 8.3. Tunnel at mile 10.6.

13.3 Continue on **State Route 410** at summit of Cayuse Pass (elevation 4694 feet) as S.R. 123 ends. *Note: Chinook Pass is uphill to the right at an elevation of 5440 feet, a worthwhile 7.2-mile round trip.* If weather is cool, put on all available clothing and plunge downhill for ten miles. Side road goes left to Sunrise at mile 17.0; to Crystal Mountain right at 21.7. Pass Dalles Campground at 28.9. Pass through Greenwater at mile 36.6; grocery and cafe. Federation Forest State Park Interpretive Center is at 38.3.

49.8 Turn left on **Mud Mountain Road** toward Mud Mountain Dam. Turn sharp right at mile 51.7 as main thoroughfare goes left into Mud Mountain Dam Park. Road bends right at mile 53.9 and is renamed **284 Avenue S.E.**

56.3 Turn right into fairgrounds; end of tour around Mt. Rainier.

MASON COUNTY

106 TWANOH–MASON LAKE

STARTING POINT: Twanoh State Park. From Seattle take Bremerton ferry; follow signs to Belfair and Twanoh State Park on State Routes 3 and 106. Park in picnic area parking lot. From the south take exit 104 from I-5 in Olympia and follow U.S. 101 and State Route 106 to Twanoh State Park.

DISTANCE: 37 to 44 miles.
TERRAIN: Hilly.
TOTAL CUMULATIVE ELEVATION GAIN: 1450 feet.
RECOMMENDED TIME OF YEAR: Avoid major summer holidays and clam tides; otherwise, any season.
RECOMMENDED STARTING TIME: 9 to 10 A.M.
ALLOW: 5 hours.
POINTS OF INTEREST
Signboard in Union commemorating Hood Canal discovery

ELEVATION PROFILE

Fog softens the silhouettes of houses nudging the southern shoreline of Hood Canal. Views of the snow-covered Olympic Mountains are not possible on this morning. The campgrounds and beaches of Twanoh State Park appear deserted. Only the sounds of screaming gulls and cawing crows fill the air as they argue over scavenging claims on the carcasses of salmon along the little stream that bisects the park.

Many black-and-white ducks (bufflehead and goldeneye) dive for food deep under the water, while large flocks of American wigeon paddle near the shoreline, frequently upending and thrusting their beaks into the shallow muddy water for a tasty morsel. Surf scoters join grebes and loons along the many bays and coves of Hood Canal. A kingfisher's rattle shatters the stillness as he lands atop a flagpole. An owl surveys the scene from a tall post. On second glance, the owl is identified as a cleverly carved wooden replica. Live cormorants sit upright on old pilings that march sporadically along the shoreline. Seals invade the cool waters, seeking their share of the fish population.

As the road climbs the hillside high above the canal the fog clears. Hundreds of acres of Christmas tree plantings, now overgrown and neglected, march over the hills and valleys. Patches of snow lie beneath evergreen huckleberry and manzanita, which flourish in the stony, sandy soil. Frosted, red-berried kinnikinnick cascades down the banks of roadway cuts. Suddenly, a red-tailed hawk swoops low across the road into the brush, comes out with empty talons, and flies up into a nearby tree.

Grandiose entrance structures advertising real-estate developments of Lake Limerick face the road along Mason Lake Drive. Trees and brush surround a little frozen puddle of a lake. Along the southwestern shore of Mason Lake a Simpson Timber Company recreation area offers relaxation for employees. Behind locked gates and nestled among virgin Douglas fir and hemlock, the park wears the chilly, neglected cloak of winter. Mason County Park and fishing access near the northeast corner of the lake is attractive for a lunch stop but posts a notice of closure from November through February.

Forest closes in as the hill between Mason Lake and Hood Canal first warms bicyclists as they climb, then cools them as they plunge toward the canal. On a winter day the last four miles of riding along Hood Canal are a bracing experience. Spring, summer, and fall will bring different sights and sounds, warmer weather, and the ebb and flow of automotive traffic.

MILEAGE LOG

0.0 Picnic area parking lot, Twanoh State Park. Leave the park and turn right (west) on **State Route 106**. Several restaurants and cafes line the highway.

7.3 Turn left and uphill on **E. McReavy Road**. A few yards farther on State Route 106 is a roadside attraction—a highway department signboard commemorating Captain George Vancouver's discovery of Hood Canal. *Note: Those with an aversion to steep hills and a tolerance of traffic may choose to continue on S.R. 106 for 3.4 miles, left on Purdy Cutoff Road 2.8 miles, left on U.S. 101 1.9 miles, then left on Brockdale. This adds 3.0 miles to total distance.* Roadway is steep at first but soon moderates and provides a view of the canal.

14.1 Continue on **E. Brockdale Road** as it enters from the right.

16.0 Turn left on **McEwan Prairie Road**. *Note: For a cafe lunch in Shelton, continue on Brockdale for 2.2 miles; turn left from left-turn lane shortly after Alpine Way goes left. Shelton is at bottom of hill 1.1 miles farther. Return to McEwan Prairie turnoff after lunch.* In spring, miniature flowers of the white erythronium lily, red paintbrush, purple violet, and yellow Oregon grape line roadsides of McEwan Prairie.

18.4 Turn left on **Mason Lake Drive** toward Mason Lake and Lake Limerick as McEwan ends. Grocery at 19.2. Lake Limerick roads go left just before and after crossing a creek under a railroad trestle at mile 19.8.

23.3 Turn left on **E. Mason Lake Drive West** toward Lake Trask. At mile 29.4 Mason County Mason Lake Park offers picnic sites, modern rest rooms and boat-launching facilities.

29.9 Turn left on **E. Trails Road** as Mason Lake Drive ends. Road undulates slightly, then dives down an unusually steep hill.

33.3 Turn left at bottom of hill on **State Route 106** and proceed along Hood Canal waterfront.

37.0 End of ride at Twanoh State Park.

107 MASON LAKE–GRAPEVIEW

STARTING POINT: Visitor's parking lot of North Mason High School, near Belfair at toe of Hood Canal. From the north take ferry from Seattle to Bremerton; follow signs through Belfair. Continue on State Route 3 uphill from Hood Canal, under concrete railroad trestle to high school entrance at top of hill. From the south take State Route 16 through Tacoma to Gorst and State Route 3 south to high school.

DISTANCE: 37 miles.
TERRAIN: Hilly.
TOTAL CUMULATIVE ELEVATION GAIN: 1500 feet.
RECOMMENDED TIME OF YEAR: Weekends, holidays, or when school is not in session.
RECOMMENDED STARTING TIME: 9 A.M.
ALLOW: 5 hours.
POINTS OF INTEREST
Waterscapes
Tree farms

ELEVATION PROFILE

Mason County, among the least populated of counties in southwestern Washington, offers many low-traffic backroads. Although the county is well removed from the direct effects of suburbia, signs of population pressure are evident in summer homes springing up around the many forest-ringed lakes. Mason Lake, one of the largest in the county, features permanent residences in addition to a county park with modern facilities.

Much of Mason County is devoted to tree farms. Good forest management practices are evident in the vigorous stands of Douglas fir, while the conical shapes of smaller, sheared trees attest to the energetic pursuit of the Christmas tree trade. Tree farms allow native shrubbery typical of the Hood Canal region to flourish. Evergreen huckleberry edges many of the roads and extends back into the forest. The glossy, green branches sought after by the florist trade command a premium, as implied by the No Brush Picking signs posted at regular intervals. Other handsome evergreen bushes that thrive in the soil of the lower Puget Sound country include the sticky laurel and the red-barked manzanita. The madrona tree, a larger relative of the manzanita, attains great size and grows abundantly along Hood Canal.

Wine and juice grapes were once an important crop cultivated on the hillsides above the inlets of lower Puget Sound, but today the winery on Stretch Island and all of the vineyards are gone. The nearby community of Allyn boasts a cafe and grocery and a delightful waterfront park for a late lunch or just a snack to fuel cyclists up the long hill to the tour's end.

MILEAGE LOG

0.0 Parking lot of North Mason High School. Go out north entrance drive, turn right on **State Route 3**, and freewheel downhill on three-foot-wide paved shoulder.

1.6 Turn left at a wye on **State Route 106** at bottom of hill. Wide, paved shoulder narrows to 18 inches or less. Grocery on right at mile 4.5. Occasional glimpses of Hood Canal through trees between homes.

5.6 Turn left and uphill on **E. Trails Road** toward Mason Lake County Park and Trails End Lake. Keep right at 7.2 as side road bears left to Trails End Lake.

9.0 Turn right on **E. Mason Lake Drive West**. Mason Lake County Park on left at mile 9.6; picnic sites, swimming, and rest rooms with hot showers.

15.7 Turn left at stop sign on **E. Mason Lake Drive** as Mason Lake Drive West ends.

17.9 Turn left and downhill on **E. Mason Lake Drive E.** The road turns right at mile 19.8, heads uphill, and is renamed **E. Mason Benson Road**.

20.6 Turn right on **E. Benson Lake Road** and follow around lake. Fishing access with toilets at mile 22.2.

22.3 Turn right on **E. Mason Benson Road** as Benson Lake Road ends.

24.2 Turn left on **State Route 3** as Mason Benson Road ends. A four-foot-wide paved shoulder eases traffic concerns.

24.8 Turn right on **Grapeview Loop Road** toward Grapeview, Stretch Island, and Treasure Island.

29.2 Turn left by Grapeview Store, fire station, and post office. Public boat launch at 29.9. *Note: The side trip to Treasure Island at mile 29.8 offers interesting seascapes.*

32.9 Turn right on **State Route 3** as Grapeview Road ends. Cross Sherwood Creek and continue on wide, paved shoulder. Grocery and cafe in Allyn at mile 33.5. Public park and pier on right by church.

33.8 Continue straight at wye as S.R. 3 veers left and uphill.

35.8 Turn left on **Victor Cutoff Road** at junction with **State Route 302**. Crank uphill through forest.

37.0 Turn right into entrance of North Mason High School athletic field parking lot. Go through lot and around gate and bear right on asphalt path.

37.3 Visitors parking lot of North Mason High School; end of tour.

108 BELFAIR–TAHUYA

STARTING POINT: Picnic area parking lot of Belfair State Park. From the Seattle area, take ferry to Bremerton and follow signs to Belfair via State Route 3. Turn right, then left (west) on State Route 300 at Belfair and continue to park entrance. From the Tacoma area, cross the Narrows Bridge on State Route 16 to Port Orchard and Gorst, then follow State Routes 3 and 300 to the park.

DISTANCE: 26 to 34 miles.
TERRAIN: Half flat, half hilly.
TOTAL CUMULATIVE ELEVATION GAIN: 1250 feet.
RECOMMENDED TIME OF YEAR: Avoid hunting seasons; otherwise, any time of year. Rhododendrons bloom from late May to early June.
RECOMMENDED STARTING TIME: 9 to 10 A.M.
ALLOW: 4 to 5 hours.
POINT OF INTEREST Views of Hood Canal

ELEVATION PROFILE

Shaped like a long, crooked finger, the narrow extension of Puget Sound known as Hood Canal gouges a swath through Mason County, with the tip of the nail just touching Belfair. Nature has created many miles of glorious salt-water shoreline to explore and enjoy. The State of Washington claims several parcels along the canal and has developed them into parks. Belfair is the most advantageous home base for exploring the north shore of these sheltered waters in the shadow of the Olympic Mountains. Captain George Vancouver discovered the canal when he sailed into Puget Sound in 1792 and named it after fellow countryman Samuel Hood. The name stuck, though the possessive "s" in Hood's has been dropped.

A steep hillside rises above the north shore road, and summer homes vie with permanent residences to fill the available space along the narrow shoreline. Fifteen miles from the park the hillside recedes, allowing more breathing room for the houses as the canal executes its great bend and heads north. Tacoma's Lake Cushman Power Plant stands out as a prominent landmark across the canal.

The calm waters of Hood Canal provide a winter home for many varieties of ducks: goldeneye, bufflehead, and surf scoter, to name a few. Gulls and shorebirds explore the shallow mud flats near estuaries of small creeks. Eventually the road along the canal's east shore loses its hard surface and becomes very narrow as it skirts a high bluff. Much of this forested bluff land belongs to the state and is managed by the Department of Natural Resources (DNR). Sustained-yield logging practices give the people of Washington a continued source of state monies for the school fund. DNR also provides recreation areas by maintaining roads and building primitive camping and picnicking sites. Land that has been clearcut is quickly cleaned of debris and replanted to Douglas fir. Stands of young noble fir for the Christmas tree trade add diversity to the ridge-top landscape. Lodgepole pine and white pine compete for toe holds with the evergreen madrona tree. The wild roadside rhododendron, flowering gem of the evergreen plant world, puts on a dazzling display of rose-pink blooms during late spring. Bright, sunny days open up vistas westward across the canal to the 6000-foot snow-covered peaks at the southern end of the Olympic Mountain range. The scenery changes with the seasons, making this an interesting tour at any time of year. Diversity is the key word for an excursion that travels from sea level to ridge crest and back again in the short span of only 34 miles.

MILEAGE LOG

0.0 Belfair State Park picnic area parking lot. Leave park and turn left (west) on **State Route 300**. The state route designation ends after 0.4 mile, and the road is named **North Shore Road**.

1.1 Bear left on **Sundstrom Road** for 0.3 mile diversion along the water, then continue on **North Shore Road**.

2.4 Bend left on **Landon Road** for another waterfront diversion, this time for 0.8 mile. **North Shore Road** crosses the estuary of Tahuya River at mile 11.1. *Note: The tour eventually goes up Belfair Tahuya Road to the right 0.1 mile beyond the bridge, but for more views of Hood Canal, continue on North Shore Road.* Tahuya offers the services of a grocery store and snack bar at mile 11.7.

15.5 Stop at bridge over Rendsland Creek, observe scenery, and turn back along North Shore Road. *Note: North of this point the road deteriorates to a single-track gravel road with excessively steep grades and is recommended only for the hardy cyclist.* Return to Tahuya at mile 19.4.

19.9 Turn left on **N.E. Belfair Tahuya Road** toward Haven Lake, Dewatto, Tahuya Valley, and Maggie Lake shortly before North Shore Road crosses the Tahuya River.

20.4 Bear right on **N.E. Tahuya River Road** as Belfair Tahuya Road forks left and heads steeply uphill toward Maggie Lake and Dewatto. Lovely displays of rhododendron and squaw grass blossoms in May.

24.6 Turn right at stop sign on **N.E. Belfair Tahuya Road**. Continue with main thoroughfare as Tee Lake Road goes left to Tee Lake at mile 25.3. Rhododendrons decorate roadsides at edge of forest.

27.2 Turn right into Howell Lake Recreation Area (DNR). Picnic tables and pit toilets.

27.9 Turn right on main road again upon leaving Howell Lake Recreation Area.

29.6 Turn right toward Belfair at T junction. Cross Tahuya River 0.3 mile beyond and continue uphill along the valley of a tributary creek. Cross Elfendahl Pass Road at mile 32.1.

33.9 Descend steep hill and turn left on **North Shore Road** as Belfair Tahuya Road ends.

34.3 Turn right into Belfair State Park entrance. Those who have not had enough exercise bicycling may go swimming in Hood Canal. Hot showers are available at the camping area rest rooms.

109 PICKERING PASSAGE

STARTING POINT: Parking area across road from Spencer Lake Tavern near Shelton in Mason County. From the north take the ferry from Seattle to Bremerton and follow signs through Belfair toward Shelton via State Route 3. Ten miles southwest of Allyn, turn left on Pickering Road toward Hartstene Island, Spencer Lake, and Phillips Lake. Continue one mile to tavern and parking area. From the south take exit 104 (U.S. 101) from I-5 to Shelton, then State Route 3 eight miles to Pickering Road turnoff.

DISTANCE: 34 miles.
TERRAIN: Hilly.
TOTAL CUMULATIVE ELEVATION GAIN: 1900 feet.
RECOMMENDED TIME OF YEAR: Avoid opening week of fishing season; otherwise, any season.
RECOMMENDED STARTING TIME: 9 to 10 A.M.
ALLOW: 4 to 5 hours.
POINTS OF INTEREST
Jarrell Cove State Park
Views of Hammersley Inlet

Perhaps to us wheel-happy landlubbers the name Pickering Passage does not ring a bell; even the name Hartstene means only an island somewhere in Puget Sound, probably not one of the San Juan group. To the boater and sailor, Pickering Passage is a narrow but important stretch of water in southern Puget Sound, between the Mason County mainland and Hartstene Island. Jarrell Cove extends from the passage into northern Hartstene Island, furnishing an ideal site for one of Washington's several marine state parks. Boaters tie up to the piers and several buoys anchored in the cove. A picnic area, rest rooms with hot showers, and a few camping sites make Jarrell Cove State Park attractive. As a marine park, however, it is not designed for the motorist; its terra firma gateway stands at the end of a narrow, bumpy, gravel road.

Until the 1950s Hartstene Island (the natives spell it *Harstine*) was accessible only by boat or by a small ferry that crossed Pickering Passage to the western side of the island. Now Pickering Road carries traffic to a new bridge, which has opened the island to more intensive development. In spite of the bridge the island is still rather sparsely settled and provides several miles of traffic-free, although hilly, bicycling.

Blackberry vines climb over a large bull rail at the edge of an old log-rafting area in a finger of Jarrell Cove. Cables hold together a ramp of small logs, providing a slide for the released logs to skid down on their way to the shallow cove below, to splash or plop, depending on the tide. Deer roam freely across Hartstene Island and understand fully the principle that the shortest distance between two points is a straight line, even if it means almost colliding with a touring bicyclist.

This bicycle tour follows roads along the shoreline of inlets and bays in

southern Puget Sound. Dense forests cover much of the landscape, allowing only fleeting glimpses of the scenery across the waters. One viewpoint at Mason County Jacoby Park encompasses the timber-industry-dominated waterfront at Shelton, Mason County seat. Across Hammersley Inlet, private residences crowd the shoreline, sending their long, steep driveways up to the access road on the hillside above. Tugboats towing barges set no speed records as they chug along at a steady five to eight knots. On the southwestern horizon Mt. Rainier is often visible.

The Pickering Passage bridge provides an excellent vantage point for marine bird-watching. Scoters, loons, grebes, and murrelets are a few of the many species that dive and find nourishment in the sheltered, productive inlets and passages of Puget Sound. Ducks preferring fresh water fly in and out of Spencer Lake, where anglers enjoy seclusion among the water lilies.

MILEAGE LOG

0.0 Parking area across road from Spencer Lake Tavern. Turn right (west) on **E. Pickering Road**.

0.9 Turn left on **E. Spencer Lake Road**. Fishing access on Spencer Lake at mile 2.0.

3.7 Turn left on **E. Agate Road** as Spencer Lake Road ends by Pioneer School.

6.0 Turn right on **E. Agate Loop** and follow it as it bends left at mile 6.5. Cross Campbell Creek, view Chapman Cove, and crank up steep hill.

7.7 Turn right on **E. Crestview Drive**. Road bends left at mile 9.7 and is renamed **E. Shorecrest Drive**. Views of Oakland Bay and Hammersley Inlet.

10.1 Turn right on **E. Shorecrest Parkway**, then right again into Mason County Jacoby (Shorecrest) Park. View the inlet and Shelton's industrial waterfront, and crank up out of the park again.

10.3 Turn left on **E. Shorecrest Parkway**, pass E. Shorecrest Drive, and turn right on **E. Kingston Way**.

10.6 Turn right at stop sign as Kingston ends. This is **E. Hillcrest Drive**.

10.7 Turn left on **E. Leeds Drive**. Views of Hammersley Inlet and Mt. Rainier.

12.0 Turn left on **E. Valley Rose Drive** as Leeds ends.

12.1 Turn right on **E. Crestview Drive**. If this intersection looks familiar, you are right. Continue on **E. Agate Road** as it joins from the left by Agate Grocery at mile 12.9. Road is renamed **E. Pickering Road** as it bends left at mile 15.8.

18.7 Turn right at wye on **E. Harstene** (sic) **Bridge Road** to Hartstene Island. After crossing bridge, turn left on **North Island Drive** toward state park.

23.0 Descend a hill and turn left on **Wingert Road** toward state park. Wingert is a narrow, winding, gravel driveway and is easy to miss.

23.8 Jarrell Cove State Park; lunch stop. If weather is inclement, a foot trail leads to a shelter on point at southwest end of park. After lunch, go back out entrance road and turn right on **North Island Drive**.

25.0   Turn left on **E. Hartstene Is. No. Rd.** by Community Hall.

28.4   Turn right on **South Island Drive** and freewheel down to near water level.

31.6   Turn left toward Hartstene Bridge and cross Pickering Passage back to mainland.

32.2   Continue on **E. Pickering Road** as it joins from the left at mile 32.2. End of tour by Spencer Lake Tavern at 34.2. If hunger persists, the Spencer Lake Tavern/Cafe offers good food and congenial atmosphere.

110 OCEAN SHORES

STARTING POINT: Ocean City State Park. From the north take exit 104 (U.S. 101) from I-5; continue on State Route 8 and U.S. 12 to Aberdeen, and U.S. 101 to Hoquiam. Continue west on State Route 109 and turn south on State Route 115 to Ocean City State Park. From the south take exit 88B (U.S. 12) from I-5; pick up U.S. 101 in Aberdeen and State Route 109 at Hoquiam. Turn left on State Route 115 to the park. Park in picnic area parking lot near registration cupola.

DISTANCE: 20 to 25 miles.
TERRAIN: Flat.
TOTAL CUMULATIVE ELEVATION GAIN: 50 feet.
RECOMMENDED TIME OF YEAR: Any season.
RECOMMENDED STARTING TIME: Anytime.
ALLOW: 3 hours.
POINTS OF INTEREST
Ocean City State Park
Grays Harbor north jetty
Passenger ferry to Westport

ELEVATION PROFILE

Only three miles south of Ocean City and 1.5 miles north of Ocean Shores, Ocean City State Park is ideally situated as a base camp from which to tour the North Beach Peninsula. As part of the natural sand spit extending southward to form the northern mandible of the mouth of Grays Harbor, the park offers grassy sand dunes and an expansive sandy beach to explore. Small, shallow, marshy lakes attract numerous waterfowl. Dense clumps of wax myrtle provide evergreen beauty in the midst of deciduous alder and willow. Many birds forage among the shrubs and trees, fascinating bird watchers at all seasons of the year. More than 100 tent sites and a few trailer hookups fan out over the campground circles, while a rustic group camp squeezes in among the vegetation between the entrance road and one of the lakes. Rest rooms with hot showers complete the amenities.

The platted resort community of Ocean Shores became an incorporated city in 1970. The planned parks and community clubhouses are completed, but many of the residential lots remain vacant. Paved, low-traffic roads crisscross the entire peninsula, while a network of canals connects Duck Lake with Minard Lake and extends throughout the peninsula. Motels, restaurants, inns, and a golf course welcome tourists and convention crowds. The Fog Festival in mid-February always attracts many visitors. Winter storms and minus tides beckon the beachcomber and clam digger to miles of gently sloping sandy beaches.

Traffic along State Route 115 is busy but disperses when it reaches the business district of Ocean Shores. As the route heads south, homes of all shapes and sizes sprout among the sand dunes. Some are landscaped with lawns, trees, and shrubs, while others are surrounded by dune grasses and driftwood. Nautical themes and decorations appeal to many of the home owners. Habitations decrease at the southern tip of the peninsula, where

the north jetty offers an opportunity to view the crashing surf as it slams into the huge man-made breakwater of rocks and boulders. Near this end of the long sand spit the State of Washington maintains a game refuge, visited occasionally by brown pelicans and yellow-billed loons. Short-eared owls and northern harriers fly low over the dunes by day, looking for mice and other small prey.

The mileage log for this tour takes the cyclist around the perimeter roads of the city of Ocean Shores, but many variations of the route may be made to shorten or lengthen the basic 20.2-mile tour. One such variation incorporates the passenger ferry between Westport and the Ocean Shores marina; operated by Grays Harbor Transit, it operates daily during summer and weekends only in late spring and early fall. Another option (when ferry is operating) is to use Twin Harbors State Park near Westport as a base camp. For the energetic and traffic-hardened cyclist, the loop tour around Grays Harbor via Aberdeen is 50 miles.

MILEAGE LOG

0.0 Picnic area parking lot, Ocean City State Park. Leave parking lot and head for the park entrance.

0.5 Turn right on **State Route 115**. Follow it right as it turns west at mile 1.6.

1.9 Turn left into Ocean Shores on **N. Point Brown Avenue**. Turn right on **Ocean Shores Boulevard N.W.** almost immediately and follow it as it bends south. Proceed along the divided street past motels and through the sparsely settled residential communities.

8.1 Bear left as divided highway ends at the southwest corner of the peninsula. *Note: A short walk past the rest rooms provides access to the protected beach and the rocky north jetty, which stretches 1600 feet out into the ocean.* Road passes sewage treatment plant as it swings north and is named **E. Ocean Shores Boulevard S.W.** Large orange navigation aids appear near the plant. As the road bears left it becomes **Sportsmens Street S.W.**

9.6 Turn right on **Greenview Avenue S.W.** *Note: Sportsmens ends 0.2 mile past Greenview.*

10.5 Turn right on **Marine View Drive S.W.** as Greenview ends. *Note: A bridge over one of the canals goes left on Tonquin Avenue S.W. at mile 11.5; vantage point for viewing ducks and grebes.* Motels, a restaurant, grocery, and marina offer services at mile 12.3; passenger ferry to Westport. Road changes name to **Discovery Avenue S.E.**

12.6 Continue straight on Discovery Avenue as Point Brown Avenue goes left. A rusting boat carrier here once transferred boats between fresh-water canal and salt-water bay.

12.7 Turn right with bike route on **Catala Avenue S.E.** past Ocean Shores Interpretive Center and informational signboard toward Community Club. Pass the clubhouse at mile 12.9.

13.1 Turn right on **Duck Lake Drive S.E.** and continue north along the eastern edge of the peninsula. Pass Chinook City Park at 14.1.

Continue on Duck Lake Drive as Overlake Drive goes left across the lake at mile 15.5, and again as bike route turns left on Albatross N.E. at mile 16.2.

17.1 Turn left on **E. Rain Street N.E.** as Duck Lake Drive is marked Dead End.

17.7 Turn right on **Shoal Street N.E.**, which is first side road on right.

17.8 Turn right on **Point Brown Avenue N.E.** as Shoal ends. Cafe.

18.3 Turn right on **State Route 115** and leave Ocean Shores. Bear left with S.R. 115 as it turns north at mile 18.6.

19.7 Turn left into Ocean City State Park.

20.2 End of tour in parking area.

"Get a bicycle!"

111 OCEAN CITY STATE PARK–TAHOLAH

STARTING POINT: Ocean City State Park. From the north take exit 104 (U.S. 101) from I-5; continue on State Route 8 and U.S. 12 to Aberdeen, and U.S. 101 to Hoquiam. Continue west on State Route 109 and turn south on State Route 115 to Ocean City State Park. From the south take exit 88B (U.S. 12) from I-5; pick up U.S. 101 in Aberdeen and State Route 109 at Hoquiam. Turn left on State Route 115 to the park. Park in picnic parking area near registration cupola.

DISTANCE: 62 miles.
TERRAIN: Easy hills with some flat.
TOTAL CUMULATIVE ELEVATION GAIN: 1550 feet.
RECOMMENDED TIME OF YEAR: September through May. Avoid minus (clam) tides and Ocean Shores' mid-February Fog Festival.
RECOMMENDED STARTING TIME: 8 A.M.
ALLOW: 7 to 9 hours.
POINTS OF INTEREST
Ocean City State Park
Pacific Ocean beaches
Quinault Indian Reservation
Cranberry bogs

ELEVATION PROFILE

Because Washington State has few roads along its coastline, a bicyclist's exposure to ocean beaches is generally brief and tantalizing. This tour explores one of the longest stretches of seaside road north of Oregon, returning via the inland creek and river valleys of coastal Washington and the northern shores of Grays Harbor.

Fine sand covers miles of Olympic Peninsula beaches and provides the perfect habitat for the much-sought-after razor clam. During the open season between October and June, thousands of people line the beaches when tides are low, hoping to harvest their limit of the elusive bivalve. Automobiles are allowed on the beach but must stay above a line marked by tall poles. Gulls keep sharp eyes on the crowds of people, hoping for a chance at their share of the harvest.

Many cabins, resorts, and motels perch along the shoreline and cluster in the several small towns catering to the tourists and clam harvesters. After crossing the Copalis River, the route climbs a bluff where tall spruce and cedar trees are sculptured into odd shapes by westerly winds. The roaring surf comes into view from high atop a steep precipice at a road turnout. Rolling terrain brings the cyclist onto the beach again, where a state park shares the limited shoreline with the little town of Pacific Beach. Just south of the Quinault Indian Reservation boundary lies Moclips, the last non-Indian town along the northern Washington coast. Indian reservations, an abandoned U.S. Coast Guard Station, and the Olympic National Park claim the remaining 80 miles.

As it enters the Quinault Indian Reservation, the route traverses a hill before returning to beach level. Beaches here are marked Tribal Property

No Trespassing, and views of the tumbling waves are blocked by a dense growth of scrub alder and salmonberry. Not until Wreck Creek is reached does the magnificent view of the ocean surf present itself. Big logs float in and out with the wave action in the creek estuary, and surf scoters frolic in the breakers.

The pleasant odor of fresh-cut cedar scents the air as the route heads downhill past the Quinault tribal cedar shake mill near the outskirts of Taholah. Lines of floats, marking the locations of gill nets for snaring salmon and steelhead, extend across the Quinault River as it flows past the village; the tribe has its own processing plant on the riverbank. After visiting this isolated cultural center, return along the shoreline to Pacific Beach, where the route heads inland. Cedar, fir, and alder trees form a dense forest, interrupted occasionally by small cedar shingle mills.

Several backroads lead past farms in the valley of the Humptulips. Great blue herons lift from the marshy sloughs. After it crosses the Humptulips River, the route turns toward the tidal-flat shoreline of the North Bay of Grays Harbor, where red-twigged cranberry bogs spread over many acres of the lowland soil.

The wide shoulder of State Route 109 allows safe pedaling of the several miles to Hogans Corner and the starting point at Ocean City State Park.

MILEAGE LOG

0.0 Ocean City State Park. Leave parking area and proceed to the park entrance.

0.3 Turn left on **State Route 115**.

1.2 Hogans Corner; cafe. Turn left with **State Route 109** as S.R. 115 ends. Pass through Ocean City at mile 3.3 and Copalis Beach at mile 6.0.

6.3 Turn left with State Route 109 and cross the Copalis River as Copalis Beach Road continues on to Copalis Crossing. Viewpoint above cliff at mile 10.4; access to beach on Roosevelt Beach Road at mile 11.4. Pacific Beach and Pacific Beach State Park on left at mile 14.7. Pass Moclips beach area at 17.0. Enter Quinault Indian Reservation at 17.7. Moclips-Olympic Highway Road goes right 20 miles to U.S. 101 at mile 17.8; includes ten miles of gravel road.

25.9 Road ends at Quinault River in Taholah. Explore village and retrace route through Moclips.

37.2 Bear right at top of hill on old highway into Pacific Beach. Pacific Beach State Park, cafe on right at 38.0.

38.1 Cross State Route 109 and continue on **Ocean Beach Road** toward Copalis Crossing and Aloha.

47.9 Continue on Ocean Beach Road toward Hoquiam and U.S. 101 in Copalis Crossing as Copalis Beach Road goes right to ocean beaches. Grocery store at this intersection. Continue straight toward Hoquiam as Kirkpatrick Road goes left to Humptulips and U.S. 101 at mile 48.6. Cross Humptulips River at 49.3.

49.6 Bear right on **Humptulips Dyke Road**, a narrow, oiled road on dike along Humptulips River. Take first left from dike as the dike road pavement ends.

50.0 Turn right on **Ocean Beach Road** again.

50.8 Bear right across old railroad grade on **Tulips**, a narrow, oiled road. A bend of the Humptulips pulls alongside 0.5 mile beyond.

51.5 Rejoin **Ocean Beach Road** and continue right.

51.7 Turn right on **Robertson Road** as the highway approaches a bridge over a creek. Robertson Road has two old railroad grade crossings and a bridge over Burg Slough.

52.7 Turn right on **Powell Road** as side road ends.

54.0 Turn right on **State Route 109** and cross Humptulips River.

54.5 Turn left on **Burrows Road** just after crossing bridge. Cross estuaries of Jessie and Campbell sloughs. Views of North Bay of Grays Harbor. Cranberry bogs butt up against road.

58.3 Turn left on **State Route 109** and continue along its wide paved shoulder.

61.0 Turn left on **State Route 115** toward Ocean Shores and Ocean City State Park at Hogans Corner.

62.0 Turn right into Ocean City State Park.

62.5 End of tour at picnic area parking lot.

One month later—

112 ABERDEEN–HOQUIAM–WISHKAH

STARTING POINT: Benn Gymnasium parking lot at Third and F streets in Aberdeen. From the north take exit 104 (U.S. 101) from I-5 and continue on State Route 8 and U.S. 12 to Aberdeen. Turn right on F Street one block after crossing bridge over Wishkah River. From the south take exit 88B (U.S. 12) from I-5 at Grand Mound and proceed west to Aberdeen. Park in parking lot except when in use by school.

DISTANCE: 29 miles. May be combined with Tour 113 (Wishkah-Wynoochee) for a total of 46 miles.
TERRAIN: Moderate.
TOTAL CUMULATIVE ELEVATION GAIN: 700 feet.
RECOMMENDED TIME OF YEAR: Any season.
RECOMMENDED STARTING TIME: 10 A.M. to 2 P.M.
ALLOW: 4 hours.
POINTS OF INTEREST
Views of Hoquiam and Wishkah rivers

ELEVATION PROFILE

Many are the cyclists who, in attempting to thread their way around the Olympic Peninsula highway loop, have found the section through Aberdeen and Hoquiam particularly hair-raising. This tour presents an entirely different aspect of the area. Rather than braving the dense traffic of U.S. 101, the route follows low-traffic, parallel side streets through the two sister cities. Where the highway is unavoidable for a half mile or so, a sidewalk provides pleasant escape from the traffic. The urban portion, however, is only a small part of the story. The rest is a delightful set of backroads along the placid, slow-moving waters of the Hoquiam and Wishkah rivers. Rows of piling in the estuarial waters, now standing idle, once anchored rafts of sawlogs, which were floated down the river. Now the mills are fed by a fleet of logging trucks thundering their way along U.S. 101, far from these quiet backroads. Two grocery stores at convenient intervals offer the customary refreshments, and their proprietors are always ready to pass the time of day with cyclists. The hills are few and relatively minor, perfect for a good afternoon workout. Just the route for a leisurely Sunday ride!

MILEAGE LOG

0.0 Benn Gymnasium parking lot at Third and F streets in Aberdeen. Proceed west on **Third Street**.
0.3 Turn right on **K Street** for two blocks.
0.4 Turn left on **Fifth Street**, which descends hill, bends left, and becomes **North Williams Street**.
0.8 Turn right on **Cherry Street**, which bends left after 1.9 miles and becomes **21st Street** in Hoquiam.
2.8 Get up on sidewalk and turn right alongside **U.S. 101**, alias **Riverside Avenue**.
3.1 Turn right on **16th Street** toward East Hoquiam and Woodlawn. Road shortly changes name to **Broadway**.

5.1 Turn right with thoroughfare as **Woodlawn Street** comes in from left. As it leaves Woodlawn, the road is renamed **East Hoquiam Road**.

14.8 Turn right by small grocery store on **Hoquiam Wishkah Road**. Cross the Wishkah River at mile 15.9.

16.5 Turn left at T junction on **Wishkah Road**.

17.2 Small grocery at corner of Wishkah Road and W. Wishkah E. Road. *Note: Owner allows bicyclists to use small park area behind store for picnic lunch in return for patronage.* After lunch, return along Wishkah Road toward Aberdeen. Pass side road toward Hoquiam at mile 17.9. As it enters Aberdeen the road is renamed **B Street**.

28.3 Turn right on **East Second Street** and continue as it jogs left on **E Street**.

28.6 Turn right on **F Street**, then left on **Third Street**.

28.7 Benn Gymnasium parking lot; end of tour.

"No, you must have made a wrong turn."

113 WISHKAH–WYNOOCHEE

STARTING POINT: Benn Gymnasium parking lot at Third and F streets in Aberdeen. From the north take exit 104 (U.S. 101) from I-5 and continue on State Route 8 and U.S. 12 to Aberdeen. Turn right on F Street one block after crossing bridge over Wishkah River. From the south take exit 88B (U.S. 12) from I-5 at Grand Mound and proceed west to Aberdeen. Park in parking lot except when in use by school.

DISTANCE: 39 miles.
TERRAIN: Moderate with one steep hill; 3.0 miles of gravel road.
TOTAL CUMULATIVE ELEVATION GAIN: 1150 feet.
RECOMMENDED TIME OF YEAR: Any season.
RECOMMENDED STARTING TIME: 10 to 11 A.M.
ALLOW: 5 hours.
POINTS OF INTEREST
Views of Wishkah, Wynoochee, and Chehalis rivers

ELEVATION PROFILE

From the busy urban atmosphere of Aberdeen to the quiet estuarial scenery of the Wishkah Valley; the mountainous, rough ridge road; the rushing, clear waters of the Wynoochee; and the swampy sloughs along the Chehalis River, this tour offers variety. It is not, however, for the beginner. Many hills, some steep and some with loose gravel on the curves, require moderate bicycling skill and stamina. For all that, it is an interesting ride. The toot of a logging donkey whistle echoes through the forest, and obscure dirt roads disappear into the trees. A glance over the side of the Wynoochee River bridge brings a glimpse of a clean, gravel river bottom through the clear, rushing waters, an ideal salmon and steelhead spawning area. A fishing access farther down the valley implies that fishermen may think so, too. A red-roofed house with many gables stands out across the valley, inviting conjecture as to its original owners.

Although the great, flowing waters of the Chehalis do not appear until near the end of the ride, their nearness is told by the meandering tidal sloughs along Devonshire Road. This narrow roadway with concrete curbing is out of place in its swampy setting; it would seem more appropriate to an urban residential area. Except for the very occasional automobile, it resembles an exclusive bicycle trail.

A brief exposure to highway traffic, ameliorated by a wide, paved shoulder, threatens to become unpleasant as the shoulder ahead disappears. At this point a dead-end side road appears, and, as is often the case, bicycles can go where automobiles cannot. By using a short railroad trestle, bicycles can detour on a smooth, blacktopped roadway through a beautiful park along the Chehalis River by the Aberdeen water pipeline. Student-generated murals decorate the retaining walls on the lower side of the highway in the park. A wood-decked walkway on the bridge over the Wishkah River provides a bicycle route across the last barrier.

MILEAGE LOG

0.0 Benn Gymnasium parking lot at Third and F streets. Head south on **N. F Street**, then left on **E. Second Street**. Continue with Second one block later as it jogs left on N. E Street.

0.4 Turn left on **B Street** and pedal out of town along Wishkah River. Road shortly is renamed **Wishkah Road**. Cross Wishkah River at mile 8.0. *Note: Route eventually turns right on side road that goes right toward Wynoochee at mile 8.7, but for lunch facilities continue on Wishkah Road.*

11.5 Thompson's Grocery at road fork. *Note: Store owner allows bicyclists to use park area behind store for picnic lunch in return for patronage.* After lunch return along Wishkah Road.

14.0 Turn left toward Wynoochee on **Wynoochee Wishkah Road**, which descends hill to creek valley, crosses creek on narrow bridge, and climbs steeply on other side; oxalis along roadside. Pavement ends at mile 15.1; summit at mile 16.5, followed by steep descent. Pavement resumes at mile 17.9 near bottom of hill.

18.7 Cross Wynoochee River and turn right on **Wynoochee Valley Road** as Wynoochee Wishkah Road ends.

24.6 Turn right on **Geissler Road** and cross Wynoochee River by fishing access. Many-gabled house on hill; morning glories along road.

25.9 Turn left on **West Wynoochee Road** as road ahead is marked Dead End. Cross U.S. 12 at mile 28.5. (On-grade crossing with central left-turn island.) Continue on other side on **Aldergrove Drive**.

29.5 Cross railroad tracks and turn right on **Devonshire Road** as Katon Road continues on. Traverse swamp on narrow concrete roadway, crossing Higgins Slough at mile 31.3, where the road is renamed **Central Park Drive**.

34.9 Cross U.S. 12 on grade and continue on **Aberdeen Lake Road** toward Lake Aberdeen. Bear left at T junction 0.1 mile thereafter. Side road goes right to Lake Aberdeen and Aberdeen Steelhead Hatchery at mile 35.1.

35.6 Turn right on **U.S. 12** and continue along wide shoulder. Beware of broken glass.

36.8 Turn left from left-turn lane on **East Sargent Boulevard** toward Junction City and Juvenile Facility. Cross railroad tracks and keep right past warehouses as road narrows and degenerates to a narrow gravel path. Get up on railroad grade, cross railroad trestle, and bear left to blacktopped path between water pipeline and the Chehalis River. Proceed through beautifully landscaped park with murals on concrete retaining walls.

38.0 Continue through mall parking lot and cross U.S. 12 at traffic light on **S. Tyler Street**. Continue left (west) on sidewalk on other side.

38.5 Cross Wishkah River on bridge walkway and immediately turn right on sidewalk along the river on other side. Cross East Market and continue on **N. E Street**.

38.7 Turn left on **E. Second Street**, then right on **N. F Street**.

38.8 Back at parking lot.

114 ELMA–SCHAFER STATE PARK

STARTING POINT: Corner of Third and Young streets in Elma. From the north take exit 104 (U.S. 101) from I-5 and continue on State Route 8 and U.S. 12 to the second Elma exit. From the south take exit 88B (U.S. 12) from I-5 at Grand Mound. Take the second Elma exit to Third Street in Elma. Park on side streets in downtown Elma.

DISTANCE: 36 to 45 miles, including three miles of unpaved road.

TERRAIN: Flat to moderate with optional hilly side trip.

TOTAL CUMULATIVE ELEVATION GAIN: Basic tour, 700 feet; side trip, 550 feet.

RECOMMENDED TIME OF YEAR: Any season. April features many spring flowers.

RECOMMENDED STARTING TIME: 9 A.M.; Sunday recommended for Satsop Nuclear Project side trip.

ALLOW: 5 to 6 hours.

POINTS OF INTEREST
Washington Public Power Supply
    System (WPPSS) Satsop Nuclear
    Project site
Schafer State Park

ELEVATION PROFILE

Being self-propelled, bicyclists are particularly conscious of personal energy production and conservation. Other forms of energy are generally of less concern, but the opportunity to view the mothballed remnants of the WPPSS Satsop Nuclear Project is too interesting to pass. To gain the view, energy must be expended to boost the masses of bicycles and bicyclists 500 feet in altitude to the abandoned parking lot next to the project. From here, the heat exchanger convection tower dwarfs the viewer with its sheer magnitude. Other nearby buildings and their spacings, viewed close up, give forcible impressions of the project's size. On the return downhill, bicyclists recover the potential energy stored in their vigorous climb.

The tour begins in Elma and follows the Chehalis River flood plain for several miles before reaching the turnoff for the side trip to the nuclear plant. The road is narrow and somewhat rough as it runs through a dairy farmyard with a milking barn on one side and riverside pastureland on the other. Jersey cows on their way to pasture stare at the two-wheeled intruders, but a few spoken words will calm them as they amble along the road. Another dairy employs the zero pasture system of feeding their Holstein-Friesian cows; served "breakfast in bed" with daily rations of freshly mowed green pasturage, the cows lounge about in their big open shelter.

The delightful rural character continues along the Satsop River, where beef cattle and horses replace the dairy herds. Several small streams flow down hillsides, cross the meadow, and empty into the meandering Satsop.

Mason County claims Schafer State Park, one of Washington State's

STAR
LAKE

LAKE
ARROWHEAD

SATSOP RIVER

MIDDLE FORK

LUNCH
STOP

PLUG MILL RD

SATSOP-CLOQUALLUM RD

SCHAFER
STATE PARK

LILLIE RD

MASON   COUNTY
GRAYS HARBOR COUNTY

COOK   CREEK

MIDDLE SATSOP RD

EAST SATSOP RD

CREEK

CLOQUALLUM RD

POWER CREEK

CLOQUALLUM

BUSH CREEK

N

8

SATSOP

START
POINT

ELMA

STAMPER RD

YOUNG FST

MAIN ST

3RD ST

2ND ST

SATSOP

4 ST

12

WAKEFIELD RD

12

RIVER

WENZEL SLOUGH RD

ABANDONED

RR   GRADE

CHEHALIS RIVER

SOUTH
ELMA

KEYES RD

SATSOP
WPPSS
NUCLEAR POWER
PROJECT

OPTIONAL
SIDE TRIP

WORKMAN CREEK RD

0   1   2   3
SCALE OF MILES

older parks. To honor the memory of John and Anna Schafer, the children of these pioneers of 1870 presented the land to the state in 1924. Huge bigleaf maple, Douglas fir, western red cedar, and western hemlock trees make the park a truly pristine setting. The large leafy foliage of the *Lobaria pulmonaria* lichen drapes the tree branches, occasionally falling to decorate the ground underneath. Water ouzels dip and bob their way over rocks and stones of the rushing East Fork of the Satsop River, which borders the park. The handsome thick masonry walls of the comfort stations display artistry of design with smooth river stones.

Wildflowers of many shapes and colors grow in profusion along the Satsop-Cloquallum Road. Especially numerous are the spring-flowering varieties, including white spring beauties, pink bleeding hearts, white trillium, yellow skunk cabbage, and green carpets of large shamrock-leafed wood sorrel with white blossoms. Foxglove, beadruby, and false Solomon's seal display their blooms in summer. The fruit of red elderberry and devil's club lend color to the forest in late summer and early fall.

Cloquallum Creek wanders through bright green pastures. Isolated homesteads, new and old, play hide-and-seek behind the forest vegetation. The route bursts upon the edge of urbanization shortly before returning to the starting point in downtown Elma.

MILEAGE LOG

0.0   Downtown Elma. Mileage log begins at the intersection of North Third Street with W. Young Street. Head south on **North Third Street**. Cross W. Main Street with traffic light at mile 0.1. Cross U.S. 12 on an overpass at mile 0.4 and continue as the road is renamed **Wakefield Road**.

0.7   Turn right toward Elma airport on **Wenzel Slough Road**. Pass Vance Creek Park at mile 1.16. Road bends left at mile 1.8; airport is to the right. Route crosses a small creek, follows the Chehalis River, and proceeds through a dairy farm milking Jersey cows. The Watch For Cattle Crossing road sign applies to bicyclists as well as autos.

5.1   Turn right on **Keyes Road** as Wenzel Slough Road ends. *Note: For a side trip to the site of the mothballed WPPSS Satsop Nuclear*

Road hazards

*Project, turn left, crossing the Chehalis River after 0.7 mile, then ride
uphill on Keyes Road for 3.1 miles to the abandoned parking lot.
Return to this corner.* Keyes Road bends right (north) and crosses
U.S. 12 on grade at mile 6.0 to enter Satsop.

6.2 Turn left on old highway from Fourth Street in Satsop. Acute-angled
railroad tracks at 6.4.

6.8 Turn right on **East Satsop Road** and start uphill. Pass cemetery at
7.1. Road surface varies from new blacktop to a rough, patchy oiled
surface. Satsop River flows along on the left. Enter Mason County at
mile 13.3.

14.4 Keep left toward Schafer State Park as Satsop-Cloquallum Road
goes right.

14.6 Turn right into Schafer State Park. Picnic area has tables beside the
East Fork Satsop River, among the trees, and in a covered rustic
shelter. The camping area on the opposite side of the road from the
picnic area has 44 campsites and hot showers. After lunch return to
the Satsop-Cloquallum Road intersection. (Mileage log allows 0.7
mile for touring the state park.)

15.5 Turn left on **Satsop-Cloquallum Road**. Many spring-blooming wildflowers grow along this road. Pavement ends at mile 17.4, but gravel
road is firm and smooth.

17.6 Keep left as side road goes right. Begin a gentle climb. Pavement
resumes at mile 20.1. Forest, meadows, and old farmhouses. Platted
development around Lake Arrowhead begins at mile 22.7; clubhouse
at 23.3.

23.8 Bear right at a wye on **Cloquallum Road** (paved) toward Elma.
Cross Cloquallum Creek several times, passing green pastures.
Enter Grays Harbor County at mile 28.6.

32.1 Bear right on unmarked road (first right turn). No road signs, but
mailboxes identify it **Stamper Road**. Top a ridge at mile 33.6 and
start a rapid descent. Cross railroad tracks at the bottom of the hill at
mile 35 as signs of civilization appear.

35.2 Road bends left, then right, and is renamed **Oakhurst Drive** and
North F Street in succession.

35.7 Turn right on **East Young Street** as F Street ends, and cross railroad
tracks on an overpass.

35.9 End of tour at starting point on North Third Street in downtown Elma.

115 ELMA–OAKVILLE

STARTING POINT: Corner of North Third and Young streets in Elma. From the north take exit 104 (U.S. 101) from I-5 and continue on State Route 8 and U.S. 12 to the second Elma exit to Third Street in Elma. From the south take exit 88B (U.S. 12) from I-5 at Grand Mound and proceed west to the second Elma exit to Third Street in Elma. Park on side streets in downtown Elma.

DISTANCE: 46 miles.
TERRAIN: Flat with one minor hill.
TOTAL CUMULATIVE ELEVATION GAIN: 500 feet.
RECOMMENDED TIME OF YEAR: Any season.
RECOMMENDED STARTING TIME: 8 to 10 A.M.
ALLOW: 5 to 6 hours.
POINT OF INTEREST
Old steam locomotive in McCleary's Beerbower Park

ELEVATION PROFILE

DISTANCE IN MILES

Elma's only traffic signal turns green, and bicycles roll down the hill, across the freeway overpass, and out into open farm country. The road is built up on fill to keep it above the not infrequent floodwaters from the Chehalis River. Previous meanderings of the river are evident in the many oxbow lakes about the landscape. Soon the river flows by underneath as the route enters the community of South Elma. An abandoned railroad grade parallels the road through dairy farms interspersed with stretches of forest. Red-winged blackbirds sing and display their brilliant orange epaulets, ducks flush from oxbow puddles, and cattle with bright red ear tags stare as bicycles whisper along. Old orchards, now serving as pasture, are neatly trimmed at cow-head height. Occasional large-wheeled irrigation systems keep the fields green for pasture and for replenishing the occasional pungent silage pile.

A carefully tended cemetery and a grange hall (the conversion of an old schoolhouse) are the only evidence of the former community of Sharon. A family-style, oyster-and-ham dinner beginning at noon on the first Saturday in April is an annual event at the Sharon Grange. As the tour continues, swampland shrubbery closes in, and hanging lichens festoon the branches. At the second crossing of the Chehalis, the route makes a brief traverse of the Chehalis Indian Reservation, and the town of Oakville appears with a shady city park for a picnic lunch. Enhancement of the lunchtime menu may be obtained from the town's grocery store and cafe on Pine Street.

After lunch, the route returns to bucolic settings by way of the backyard of a sawmill and log yard. The mighty Chehalis rolls by, its banks occasionally penetrated by fishermen's trails. A brief reappearance of valley farms is cut short by increasing proximity of the river to the edge of the valley, whereupon the only remaining bicycle route lies along the broad shoulder of the highway. Soon another escape route presents itself as a backroad wending its way up Mox Chehalis Creek. A diamond-shaped

highway sign with a black cow silhouette gives warning of possible road hazards. Power lines hum briefly overhead as cattle ranches march up the hillsides.

In McCleary's Beerbower Park, an old wood-burning steam locomotive and fire pumper inject a nostalgia theme. During McCleary's Bear Festival in July, the nostalgia turns to celebration, featuring bear stew. Automotive traffic picks up again until another escape route is found, leading into Elma via the back door by the Grays Harbor County Fairgrounds. A few blocks of side streets are all that remain of this tour through the Chehalis Valley. While in Elma, take time to view the large murals that cover entire walls of buildings and depict the old logging days of Grays Harbor County.

MILEAGE LOG

0.0 Starting from the corner of North Third Street and West Young Street in Elma, head south on **North Third Street** and cross U.S. 12 on overpass. Continue across valley and over the Chehalis River.

1.9 Cross the Chehalis River and turn left with **South Bank Road** in South Elma as Workman Creek Road goes right.

7.3 Bear right at a wye with South Bank Road. Sharon Grange is on the right at 7.9, and Sharon Cemetery on the left at mile 8.1.

16.0 Bear left as Garrard Creek Road goes right. Cross Chehalis River and continue through Chehalis Indian Reservation.

17.4 Bear left with main thoroughfare on Oakville Road as Oakville Cemetery Road goes right. As it enters Oakville the road is named **State Street**. Oakville city park on right at mile 17.8.

17.9 Turn left on **Pine Street (U.S. 12)** by post office in Oakville.

18.2 Turn right on **N. Park Street** across from drive-in cafe and milepost 35. Skirt a forest products log yard and mill.

18.7 Bear right on **U.S. 12**, then cross shortly and continue on a narrow, oiled road along Chehalis River. This is **Elma Gate Road**.

23.3 Join **U.S. 12** as Elma Gate Road ends. Cross and continue on shoulder, which varies from two to six feet. Grocery in Porter on right at mile 26.1.

27.9 Cross Mox Chehalis Creek and turn right by grocery in Malone. Continue up creek valley on **Mox Chehalis Road**. Power lines overhead at mile 31.0.

35.9 Bear left with Mox Chehalis Road as Mox Chehalis E. Road goes right. Cross State Route 8 at mile 36.6.

36.8 Turn left on **William McCleary Road** and continue over hill into McCleary as road is renamed **3rd Street**.

37.3 Turn left on **Simpson Avenue (State Route 108)**. Beerbower Park on right. Cafe, grocery, bakery.

38.4 Continue straight toward Whites on **Elma McCleary Road** as S.R. 108 goes left to Olympia, Elma, and Aberdeen.

38.6 Continue straight on **Church Road** as Elma McCleary Road bends left by grocery and auto repair shop.

39.1 Bear left on **Elma Hicklin Road** as Church Road ends.

40.3 Cross railroad tracks and bear right on **Elma McCleary Road** as

Elma Hicklin Road ends.

41.9 Pass Hicklin Road as it forks to the right and turn left on **Heise Road**. Cross Wildcat Creek. Cross State Route 8 on grade at mile 42.4, and continue past highway rest area.

43.3 Turn right on **S. Union Road** as Heise Road ends and Abbott Road continues but is marked Dead End. Cross State Route 8 again and continue on **Fairground Road** past Grays Harbor County Fairgrounds.

45.0 Cross Elma-Oakville Road and continue on **Menzel Haverly Road** as Fairground Road ends.

45.3 Turn left on **Stamper Road** as Menzel Haverly Road ends. Road executes several bends threading its way through residential area, and is renamed **Oakhurst Drive** and **North F Street** in succession.

46.0 Turn right on **East Young Street** as F Street ends.

46.3 End of tour at North Third Street in Elma.

*"I can climb **any** hill with this!"*

116 OAKVILLE–BROOKLYN–MONTESANO

STARTING POINT: City park by corner of Main and State streets in Oakville. Take exit 88B (U.S. 12 West) from I-5 to Oakville. Park on side streets near city park.

DISTANCE: 73 miles.
TERRAIN: Mountainous to flat, with 7.5 miles of gravel road.
TOTAL CUMULATIVE ELEVATION GAIN: 1400 to 2000 feet.
RECOMMENDED TIME OF YEAR: Avoid snow or spring thaw; otherwise, any season.
RECOMMENDED STARTING TIME: Start early enough to allow sufficient daylight to complete tour.
ALLOW: 8 to 10 hours or overnight.
POINTS OF INTEREST
Ridge crest scenery
WPPSS Satsop Nuclear Project

ELEVATION PROFILE

DISTANCE IN MILES

DISTANCE IN MILES

Logging, one of the principal industries in Grays Harbor County, began soon after the arrival of settlers of European extraction in the 1850s. The great forests of Douglas fir, hemlock, and cedar echoed with the sounds of "timbe-r-rr," as one giant tree after another crashed to the forest floor. Today, the virgin stands of timber are gone and even much of the second growth has been harvested. Douglas fir, which grows so well in the mild, wet climate of the Pacific Northwest, is now a valuable crop, planted with care and harvested on a regular basis.

Lumberjacks of yesteryear lived lonely, isolated lives: the logging camps, with rude bunkhouses and few comforts, sprang up close to the working area, and only occasionally did the loggers get out for a night on the town. Things are different today as loggers live with their families in small towns and commute many miles to work, just as urban dwellers do. Most of the old logging camps disappeared completely many years ago, but an occasional small community still clings to life. Nestled in the valley of the North River in the Willapa Hills east of Raymond, Brooklyn is still home to a few families. It even boasts of a school for approximately 90 children in grades K through 12. But the old bunkhouses and other buildings associated with early logging have been dismantled or lie buried beneath a tangled growth of brambles. The last remaining business establishment, an old tavern in continuous operation since 1933, burned down in 1991, leaving the town without a grocery store or cafe. The closest food supply now is in Artic, 17 miles away.

Although involving several miles of gravel roads, this tour into the hills east of Brooklyn offers the bicyclist a close look at a well-managed forest replanted to Douglas fir. Deer roam the hillsides, seeking the browse offered by the young forest. Views from the long, narrow ridge crest include Mt. Rainier and vapor plumes from the steam electric power plant at Centralia.

Along the road beside the North River, traffic is almost nonexistent. Red-tailed hawks survey the parklike setting of alders, bigleaf maples, and green grass, while ruffed grouse flush from clumps of brush. Homes are few and far between. Forested scenery continues along State Route 107 with increasing traffic density as Montesano and Elma are approached. Lake Sylvia State Park, just up the hill from motels in Montesano, boasts a fine swimming beach, secluded campsites, and a comfortable group camp area available by reservation with the park manager.

Once past Elma, the route branches on rural roads along the Chehalis River, where pastureland and dairy farms spread across the valley. Stunted Garry oak trees, growing in the area that was once an Indian campground, give their name to the little town of Oakville on the edge of the Chehalis Indian Reservation.

MILEAGE LOG

0.0 Oakville city park by corner of Main and State streets in Oakville. Head south (away from highway) on **State Street**.

0.5 Bear right at road junction and proceed through Chehalis Indian Reservation.

1.9 Cross Chehalis River and turn left on **Garrard Creek Road** across bridge over railroad cut.

5.3 Bear right toward Brooklyn as Garrard Creek Road bends left toward Centralia. Pavement ends at mile 8.5. Climb steep hill, gaining summit ridge at about mile 10.4. Pavement resumes at mile 16.2 after long descent.

19.7 Bear right with **North River Road** as unpaved Smith Creek Road goes left to Raymond. Riverbank by bridge over North River offers possible picnic site at mile 20.4 as road enters Grays Harbor County.

32.8 Turn right on **Artic Road** as North River Road approaches new concrete bridge over North River.

35.1 Bear right on **U.S. Highway 101** by Artic Grocery and Tavern. Restaurant on right at mile 36.2.

36.9 Turn right at wye on **State Route 107** toward Montesano, just past highway weighing station. Cross Chehalis River at mile 44.0. Beware of dangerous railroad grade crossing after leaving bridge. *Note: Boat Launch Road leads sharp right to fishing access with toilets.* As it enters Montesano, the road is named **Main Street**.

45.0 Turn right on **Pioneer Avenue** at traffic light in Montesano. Motel, cafes, bakery. *Note: For an overnight stay at Lake Sylvia State Park, turn left here, then right and uphill on Third Street; two miles and 250-foot elevation gain to the park.*

47.1 Turn right on **Monte Brady Road**, cross U.S. 12, and bear left with main thoroughfare at T junction as a dead-end road goes right.

49.7   Turn left with Monte Brady Road as Brady Loop Road continues on. Cross U.S. 12, cross railroad tracks, and bear right past grange hall on **Old Monte Brady Road**.

50.2   Bear right on **Monte Elma Road**. Cross Satsop River at mile 50.8 and continue through Satsop to Elma. *Note: Alternate route goes right at mile 51.5 in Satsop on 4 Street, continuing on Keyes Road uphill past Washington Public Power Supply System's mothballed nuclear power project, left toward Elma at stop sign at bottom of hill, rejoining route at mileage log 57.2. Adds 1.2 miles and a 600-foot elevation gain.* Drive-in restaurant in Elma at mile 55.1.

55.4   Turn right toward freeway on **Third Street** at traffic light. Cross U.S. 12 on overpass and continue across valley.

57.2   Cross Chehalis River and railroad tracks, and bend left on **South Bank Road** as side road goes right to Satsop Nuclear Project.

62.6   Bear right with South Bank Road as steel truss bridge appears ahead. Sharon Cemetery on the left at mile 63.4.

71.2   Bear left toward Oakville as Garrard Creek Road goes right to Brooklyn. Cross Chehalis River and continue through Chehalis Indian Reservation.

73.1   End of tour by city park in Oakville.

"You go on — I'm staying here tonight."

117 STEAMBOAT ISLAND

STARTING POINT: Take exit 104 (U.S. 101) from I-5 at Olympia. Follow U.S. 101 7.7 miles to Steamboat Island Road exit. Park in Griffin Elementary School parking area (nonschool days only), just off Steamboat Island Road N.W. on 33 Avenue N.W.

DISTANCE: 25 to 31 miles.
TERRAIN: Hilly.
TOTAL CUMULATIVE ELEVATION GAIN: 900 feet.
RECOMMENDED TIME OF YEAR: Any season.
RECOMMENDED STARTING TIME: 9 to 10 A.M.
ALLOW: 3 to 5 hours.
POINTS OF INTEREST
Puget Sound waterscapes
Frye Cove County Park

ELEVATION PROFILE

The name for this ride is derived from a diminutive mound of earth at the end of a long peninsula jutting into the southern end of Puget Sound. A one-lane concrete causeway across a gravel bar provides access from the mainland to the island, where houses crowd each other wall-to-wall for a piece of the highly prized waterfront. Although the island itself is of only passing interest to cycle tourists, the views across the sheltered waters to nearby islands and other peninsulas are unusual. Quiet, moderately hilly backroads offer leisurely cycling. A 90-acre tract of land at Frye Cove, acquired several years ago by Thurston County for a public park, was developed in 1991, adding toilets, delightful picnic areas, and a network of bark-surfaced trails. The only drawback is the apparent lack of potable water. With winter's high tides, loons and cormorants surface close to shore, scolding loudly about the humans occupying their secluded beach and cove. At unusually low tides, clam diggers populate the beach. A side trip to Oyster Bay adds several miles and another view of one of Puget Sound's extremities to this 25-mile tour. For the bicycle tourist not looking for a marathon spectacular, this is an enjoyable ride.

MILEAGE LOG

0.0 Parking lot of Griffin Elementary School. Proceed out of schoolyard on **33rd Avenue N.W.** to **Steamboat Island Road N.W.** and turn right. Grocery on left at mile 4.8. Cross bridge to Steamboat Island at mile 9.1. Continue on **Steamboat Island Loop N.W.**

9.5 Road doubles back at north end of island by Olympia Outboard Club Park (private). Continue around loop and back across bridge onto **Steamboat Island Road N.W.**

12.0 Go straight on **Urquhart Road N.W.** past fire station and Rignall Hall.

12.1 Bear right at wye and continue on **81st Avenue N.W.** Cross Steamboat Island Road N.W.

12.7 Road bends left and is renamed **Howe Street N.W.**

STEAMBOAT ISLAND

PUGET SOUND

STEAMBOAT IS. RD NW

MASON COUNTY
THURSTON COUNTY

KAMILCHE POINT

ARCADIA

GALLAGHER COVE

81 AVE NW

HOWE ST NW

URQUHART RD NW

SKOOKUM INLET

KEN RD

GALLAGHER COVE RD NW

STEAMBOAT IS. RD NW

OLYMPIC ST NW

YOUNG RD NW

TAYLOR RD NW

69 AVE NW

61 AVE NW

GIDDINGS RD NW

YOUNG RD NW

COUNTY PARK

FRYE COVE

TOTTEN INLET

GRAVELLY BEACH LOOP NW

ROAD NW

GRAVELLY BEACH

BURNS COVE

OYSTER BAY RD

SCOTT RD

KEATING RD

YOUNG COVE

ELD INLET

OYSTER BAY RD

41 AVE NW

SUNRISE BEACH RD

BUDD INLET

SCHNEIDER CREEK

101

OLD 101 HWY NW

STEAMBOAT IS. RD NW

33RD AVE NW

START POINT GRIFFIN SCHOOL

ROCKY PT

N

101

TO OLYMPIA

0   1   2   3
SCALE OF MILES

13.0 Rejoin **Steamboat Island Road N.W.**

13.1 Bear left on **Young Road N.W.**

15.3 Turn left on **61st Avenue N.W.** Road descends to creek bottom and climbs steeply on other side.

15.8 Turn right into entrance of Thurston County's Frye Cove Park.

16.0 Turn left by parking lot down steep, 0.1-mile paved trail to beach. Toilets and picnic facilities at bottom. Have a nice picnic lunch, pack up all trash, and retrace route to Young Road.

17.0 Turn left on **Young Road N.W.** as 61st Avenue N.W. ends.

17.6 Turn left on **Gravelly Beach Loop N.W.** as Young Road ends. Continue around point over a series of hills and dales.

20.8 Turn left on **Gravelly Beach Road N.W.** as the loop road ends. End of Young Cove appears on left.

22.3 Bear left on **Steamboat Island Road N.W.** by power substation, then immediately turn right on **41st Avenue N.W.**

23.4 Turn left on **Oyster Bay Road N.W.** as 41st Avenue ends. *Note: For an interesting side trip, turn right on Oyster Bay Road 3.0 miles to end of road and return.*

23.8 Cross U.S. 101 and continue on **Old 101 Highway N.W.** as it bends left.

24.6 Cross U.S. 101 again and turn left on **Sexton Drive N.W.**

24.7 Bear right with thoroughfare on **Steamboat Island Road N.W.**

24.8 Turn right on **33 Avenue N.W.**, then left into schoolyard. End of tour.

"Good thing it was a tree he hit — he didn't have his helmet on."

118 PRIEST POINT–TOLMIE STATE PARK

STARTING POINT: Priest Point Park in Olympia. Take exit 105B (Olympia) from I-5 and continue through city center on Plum Street, which changes its name to East Bay Drive as it leaves metropolitan area. Park entrance is two miles from I-5 exit and appears on the right about 50 yards before park road overpass. Park cars by county shops behind picnic shelter.

DISTANCE: 37 miles plus 12 miles of optional side trips.
TERRAIN: Hilly.
TOTAL CUMULATIVE ELEVATION GAIN: 1750 feet plus optional side trips totaling 350 feet.
RECOMMENDED TIME OF YEAR: Any season.
RECOMMENDED STARTING TIME: 9 A.M.
ALLOW: 5 to 7 hours.
POINTS OF INTEREST
Thurston County's Burfoot Park
Tolmie State Park

Numerous, long, fingerlike projections of land reach into southern Puget Sound to form many inlets, bays, and passages. Olympia, the capital city of Washington State, stands at the end of one of the larger inlets, Budd Inlet. Olympia's Priest Point Park fronts the inlet with forested hillside picnicking areas and is the starting point for this tour. Thurston County's Burfoot Park on Budd Inlet is a day-use park featuring nature trails, picnicking, and beach access. Several walk-in campsites with a communal fire circle are available for overnight group camping by reservation with the park manager. Other seascapes dot this tour. At Boston Harbor, a marina and small grocery cater to the boating fraternity. At Woodard Bay, mud flats are in a continuous state of flux as the tides ebb and flow into the long, narrow bay. Great blue herons frequent the shallow waters, while gulls make regular inspection flights.

Fronting on Nisqually Reach, Tolmie State Park offers views toward Anderson Island and Longbranch Peninsula in Pierce County. Although the park has no overnight camping, it offers two picnic areas, each with its own rest rooms and kitchen shelter. The kitchen facilities are equipped with stainless steel sinks, hot and cold running water, and coin-operated electric hot plates. The hillside picnic area features secluded picnic sites overlooking the sound. The beach-level shelter stands on a small knoll with paved paths down to the high-tide mark. Scuba divers find the extensive shallow beach a prime area for their sport.

Automobile traffic along most of this tour is minimal, the only busy traffic occurring on Marvin Road where it crosses I-5 and becomes State Route 510. Scenery for the most part is semirural-suburban. Evergreen huckleberry, growing in the forest edge along some of the roads, is a relatively uncommon bush, but other flora are typical of western Washington.

Commerce and industry are also represented on this tour, which includes a mushroom farm at the corner of Marvin Road and Steilacoom Road, where large piles of baled straw surround the windowless buildings. Sand and gravel companies mine the valuable aggregates just north of I-5 on Carpenter Road, but their trucks usually do not operate on weekends.

Suburbia briefly takes over as the tour approaches Olympia's city limits, to be followed by dense forest along Ames Road. A short stretch marked "Bike Route" returns the tour to the starting point at Priest Point Park.

MILEAGE LOG

0.0 Parking area behind picnic shelter in Olympia's Priest Point Park. Cross park overpass and bear right on drive on other side.

0.1 Bear left on sidewalk along **East Bay Drive**.

0.3 Cross East Bay Drive as Ames Road intersects on the right. Continue north along East Bay Drive on marked bikeway, which proceeds 0.3 mile to end at city limit, where the road is renamed **Boston Harbor Road N.E.** Continue on wide, paved shoulder. *Note: Tour may be shortened by eight miles by turning right on Woodard Bay Road at mile 3.5. Thurston County's Burfoot Park on the left at mile 4.8.*

5.3 Turn left on **73rd Avenue N.E.** for a view off Dofflemeyer Point. Grocery and marina. Return to Boston Harbor Road and continue on 73rd Avenue N.E.

6.6 Turn left on **Zangle Road N.E.** as 73rd Avenue ends by fire station. Road bends right and left and is renamed **76th Avenue N.E.** and **Zangle Road N.E.**

7.6 Turn right on **81st Avenue N.E.** as Zangle is marked Dead End.

8.7 Turn right on **Libby Road N.E.** *Note: Turning left here provides optional 3.8-mile side trip around Fishtrap Loop Road on Dickenson Point.*

10.4 Turn left on **Woodard Bay Road N.E.** Bear left with Woodard Bay Road as Lemon Road goes right at mile 11.1.

11.5 Bear right on **Shincke Road N.E.** as it comes in from a dead end on the left.

12.1 Turn left on **56th Avenue N.E.**, which rounds a bend 0.4 mile farther and is renamed **Sleater Kinney Road N.E.**

14.1 Turn left on **South Bay Road N.E.** (busy, but has wide, paved shoulders). As it rounds the end of Henderson Inlet it is renamed **Johnson Point Road N.E.**

15.5 Turn right on **Puget Road N.E.** *Note: Tour may be extended by 8.3 miles by continuing on Johnson Point Road, going around the loop on Johnson Point, and proceeding via 78th Avenue N.E. and Marvin Road to rejoin main tour at mile 17.6.*

17.1 Turn right on **63rd Avenue N.E.** as Puget Road ends.

17.8 Turn right on **Puget Beach Road N.E.**, which bends left 0.8 mile farther and is renamed **56th Avenue N.E.**

19.0 Continue on 56th Avenue N.E. as main thoroughfare turns right and is renamed Marvin Road N.E. 56th Avenue soon bends left and is renamed **Hill Road N.E.**

DICKENSON POINT

BIG FISHTRAP

FISHTRAP LOOP RD

DOFFLEMEYER POINT

DOVER POINT

ZANGLE COVE

MARINE DR

81 AVE NE

BOSTON HARBOR

76 AVE NE

SHORE ACRES RD

73 AVE NE

ZANGLE RD NE

LIBBY RD NE

RD NE

WHITHAM RD

WOODARD BAY

RD

HENDERSON INLET

JOHNSON PT. LOOP RD

MILL BIGHT

78 AVE NE

73 AVE NE

NISQUALLY REACH

JOHNSON POINT RD NE

MARVIN RD NE

PUGET BEACH RD NE

63 AVE NE

TOLMIE STATE PARK

61 AVE NE

HILL RD NE

BURFOOT THURSTON COUNTY PARK

BOSTON HARBOR RD NE

56 AVE NE

56 AVE NE

BUDD INLET

SHINCKE RD NE

LEMON RD NE

LIBBY RD

46 AVE

SLEATER KINNEY RD NE

PUGET RD NE

SOUTH BAY

HAWKS PRAIRIE RD

MARVIN RD NE

36 AVE NE

SOUTH BAY RD NE

BAY DR NE

START POINT

26 AVE NE

26 AVE NE

CARPENTER RD

HOGUM BAY RD

GULL HBR RD

AMES RD NE

PRIEST POINT PARK

21 AVE

SOUTH BAY RD

JOHN LILLY RD

SLEATER KINNEY RD NE

ABERNETHY ST NE

15 AVE NE

DRAHAM RD SE

MARTIN WAY

MARVIN RD SE

EAST BAY DR

4TH AVE

MARTIN WAY

PACIFIC

AVE

LACEY

LAKE LOIS RD

CARPENTER RD SE

6 AVE SE

KINWOOD RD

PACIFIC AVE SE

STEILACOOM RD SE

510

OLYMPIA

5

0   1   2   3

SCALE OF MILES

105

20.0   Bear left toward Tolmie State Park on **61st Avenue N.E.**, which enters park boundary in 0.2 mile. For a visit to beach area, do not turn into upper-level parking lot, but continue on main thoroughfare down steep hill.

20.5   End of road and trail system at beach; suggested lunch stop. Rest rooms and picnic shelter facilities at both upper and lower levels of park. Views of Case Inlet, Key Peninsula, and Anderson Island. Return via entrance route along **61st Avenue, Hill Road N.E.**, and **56th Avenue N.E.** to Marvin Road intersection.

22.0   Turn left on **Marvin Road N.E.** at wye. I-5 roars underneath at mile 25.9; restaurants. Drive-in cafe at Martin Way crossing at mile 26.3 as road name changes to **Marvin Road S.E.** and **State Route 510** signs appear.

27.0   Turn right on **Steilacoom Road S.E.**

27.9   Merge with **Pacific Avenue S.E.** and continue on broad, paved shoulder.

28.4   Turn right on **Lake Lois Road** about 0.1 mile past tavern. Road bends left and is renamed **6th Avenue S.E.**

28.9   Turn right on **Carpenter Road S.E.** as 6th Avenue ends. Cross Martin Way on grade and I-5 on overpass.

30.5   Bear left with main thoroughfare on **Draham Road N.E.** as Carpenter Road N.E. bends right. As Draham Road rounds a bend 0.5 mile farther, it is renamed **15th Avenue N.E.**

32.1   Turn right on **Abernethy Street N.E.**

32.8   Turn left on **26th Avenue N.E.** as Abernethy ends.

34.1   Turn left on **South Bay Road N.E.** as 26th Avenue ends, then right again on **26th Avenue N.E.**

35.7   Turn right on **Gull Harbor Road N.E.** as 26th Avenue is marked Dead End.

36.1   Turn left on **Ames Road N.E.** as Gull Harbor Road starts down a short hill. Olympia city limits.

36.5   Cross **East Bay Drive**, turn left, and continue on marked bikeway.

36.7   Bear right on drive into Priest Point Park. Cross overpass and continue to parking area by county shops to complete this tour.

119 MILLERSYLVANIA–DELPHI–OLYMPIA

STARTING POINT: Millersylvania State Park. Take exit 95 (State Route 121 North, Littlerock, Maytown) from I-5. Follow S.R. 121 to Millersylvania State Park, 3.5 miles northeast of the freeway. Park in the Kitchen #1 picnic area parking lot.

DISTANCE: 42 miles.
TERRAIN: Moderate.
TOTAL CUMULATIVE ELEVATION GAIN: 1200 feet.
RECOMMENDED TIME OF YEAR: Any season.
RECOMMENDED STARTING TIME: 9 to 10 A.M.
ALLOW: 5 to 6 hours.
POINTS OF INTEREST
McLane Creek Nature Trail
Capitol Lake Park
Olympia Brewery

ELEVATION PROFILE

Tour 47 (Millersylvania-Olympia) in *Bicycling the Backroads Around Puget Sound* also begins at Millersylvania State Park and touches some of the same places as this tour, but the two routes are quite different. This tour is six miles longer and proceeds through the town of Littlerock and the small communities of Delphi and McLane as well as the Evergreen State College campus. The route then goes through some of Olympia's residential areas, skirts its business district, and continues past Capitol Lake and the Olympia Brewery and out into the countryside of East Olympia before returning to the state park.

The McLane Creek Nature Trail, managed by the Department of Natural Resources (DNR), winds through a portion of a forested lowland valley. It gives the visitor a chance to study some natural events that change the environment: the flooding of a creek valley, the construction of beaver dams, and forest fires. Conversely, Capitol Lake and the surrounding park show how people alter the environment by changing the course of a river, damming it, and forming a lake. Marshy areas formed around the edge of the lake attract waterfowl to feed. Parks built on the dredged landfill boast picnic tables, rest rooms, and green lawns, where coots, mallards, wigeons and gulls frequently forage. An artificially introduced run of Chinook salmon makes its annual pilgrimage through Capitol Lake and up the Deschutes River to spawn.

A series of artesian wells dots the golf course near the Deschutes River at Tumwater Falls, providing the many gallons of water needed for the Olympia Brewery. Interesting guided tours take the public through the different operations in the plant. Several cemeteries along Cleveland Avenue in Tumwater beautify the environment with carefully maintained and landscaped memorial grounds and gardens.

Only small stands of evergreen trees remain in the fields and pastures of East Olympia. Not until the boundary of Millersylvania State Park is approached can the cyclist realize how the area must have appeared to the early settlers: large Douglas fir trees interspersed with hemlock and cedar tower above the brushy vine maple, salmonberry, salal, sword ferns, and many wildflowers carpeting the ground. The character of the old-growth forests has been preserved at Millersylvania State Park, because John L. Miller, the original owner of most of the land, did not clearcut the forests as did many of his neighbors, and thus left a legacy of tall timber for succeeding generations to enjoy.

MILEAGE LOG

0.0 Head out park entrance road from picnic area parking lot of Millersylvania State Park.

0.2 Turn right on **Tilley Road S. (State Route 121)** at park entrance.

0.9 Cross railroad tracks and turn right with S.R. 121 on **Maytown Road S.W.**

3.6 Go under I-5 and turn right with Maytown Road at stop sign as paved shoulder begins. Continue straight at stop sign through Littlerock at mile 6.5.

6.6 Cross railroad tracks and immediately turn right on **La France Road S.W.**

7.2 Turn left on **123 Avenue S.W.** as La France ends. Cross Black River. Road bends right at mile 7.4 and becomes **Endicott Road S.W.** Road bends right again at mile 8.8 and is renamed **110 Avenue S.W.**

9.3 Turn left on **Delphi Road S.W.** as 110 Avenue continues on. Pass through Delphi at mile 13.5.

15.7 Turn left on drive into McLane Creek Nature Trail recreation area (Washington State DNR).

16.2 End of road in parking lot by trailhead. Suggested picnic lunch stop. Pit toilets, picnic tables, guiding pamphlets for trail around beaver pond. Return to Delphi Road.

16.6 Turn left on **Delphi Road S.W.** Pass through McLane at mile 18.1.

18.6 Bear right as truck route goes left. Cross U.S. 101 on overpass at mile 19.5.

19.9 Turn right on **Mud Bay Highway S.W.**

20.2 Go past Evergreen State College entrance and turn left by fire hall on **Overhulse Road S.W.**, then immediately left on **2nd Avenue S.W.**, marked Dead End. Continue through concrete wicket on bike trail.

21.3 Turn right through concrete wicket on roadway. No street name sign here, but this is **17th Avenue N.W.**

21.6 Turn right on **Overhulse Road N.W.** as 17th Avenue ends.

22.0 Turn left on **11th Avenue N.W.**

22.5 Turn left on **Kaiser Road N.W.** as 11th Avenue ends.

22.7 Turn right on **14th Avenue N.W.** by power substation. Cross Cooper Point Road.

24.5 Turn right on **Division Street N.W.** Bicycle lane along shoulder. Bike lane ends 0.5 mile farther as roadway widens. Cross Harrison Avenue at traffic light at mile 25.1.

25.2 Turn left on **4th Avenue W.** and proceed down a hill.

25.9 Turn right at Right Turn Only sign and continue down the hill. Sidewalk available.

26.0 Turn sharp right on **5th Avenue N.** *Note: Turning left here leads to the Olympia business district, Capitol grounds, stores, and cafes.* As it proceeds around Capitol Lake, 5th Avenue changes name to **Deschutes Parkway**. Capitol Lake Park south area on left at mile 27.0; picnic tables, toilet facilities. Crosby House Museum on left at mile 28.3.

28.2 Turn left on **Boston Street S.W.** across low bridge over the Deschutes River toward the Olympia Brewery. View of Deschutes Falls.

28.4 Turn right on **Custer Way** and continue uphill. *Note: Drive leads right at mile 28.9 to Olympia Brewery visitors' entrance; guided tours of brewery.*

28.7 Cross Capitol Boulevard and take next right turn on **Cleveland Avenue** toward Yelm and Rainier. Views of golf course with brewery artesian wells on right, Oddfellows Cemetery on left. Road bends left and is renamed **Yelm Highway S.E.** Wide shoulder begins at mile 30.2.

31.5 Turn right at traffic light on **Rich Road S.E.** toward East Olympia.

32.3 Go straight on **Rixie Street S.E.** and cross railroad tracks as Rich Road bends left. Road zigzags and is renamed **78th Avenue S.E.**, **Ayer Street**, and **83rd Avenue S.E.** in quick succession.

34.6 Turn right on **Rich Road S.E.** by East Olympia store and post office. Cross railroad tracks. Cross Deschutes River at mile 37.0 and mainline railroad tracks at 37.1.

37.2 Turn left on **Old 99 Highway S.E.** as Rich Road ends.

38.1 Turn right on **McCorkle Road S.E.**, which executes a bend after 0.4 mile and becomes **113 Avenue S.E.** Crank over a hill.

40.7 Turn left on **Tilley Road S.**

41.7 Turn right into entrance of Millersylvania State Park.

41.8 Picnic area parking lot; end of tour.

"CHAARGE!"

120 BLACK RIVER

STARTING POINT: Millersylvania State Park. Take exit 95 (State Route 121 North, Maytown, Littlerock) from I-5 and follow S.R. 121 to the state park entrance, 3.5 miles northeast of the interchange. Park in Kitchen #1 picnic area parking lot.

DISTANCE: 30 miles.
TERRAIN: Flat.
TOTAL CUMULATIVE ELEVATION GAIN: 300 feet.
RECOMMENDED TIME OF YEAR: Any season; May and June best for flowers.
RECOMMENDED STARTING TIME: 10 A.M.
ALLOW: 4 to 5 hours.
POINTS OF INTEREST
Spring flowers
Historical monuments
Scatter Creek Game Range

ELEVATION PROFILE

DISTANCE IN MILES

The soil south of Olympia and north of Centralia between the Willapa Hills and Cascade foothills contains the rocky debris left by the once huge glaciers that gouged out the Puget Sound Basin. Trees grow well in this stony soil, but the usual thick underbrush of the Puget Sound forest is missing. In its place are flowers and plants, many not common to other places around western Washington. Camas lily, a deep-seated bulb, blooms April to June with predominantly blue, hyacinthlike flowers, though white ones also occur. Its bulb was an important food in the diet of the western Indians. A poisonous white-flowered bulb, resembling the camas and appropriately called the death camas, also grows in the same area, its showy flowers forming a tight terminal raceme rather than the loose one of the blue camas.

The prairie north of Rochester becomes a scene of many colors in springtime as wildflowers put on their show: orange honeysuckle, lavender vetch, blue campanula, red columbine, blue-eyed grass, pink kinnikinnick, yellow cinquefoil, blue lupine, pink roses, and yellow balsam root.

Brush and flowers preferring a moist and shady habitat thrive along the slowly moving Black River. The young purplish red twigs of the western dogwood add a touch of color to the tangle of branches along the stream. Steeple bush produces soft pyramidal clusters of bright pink flowers in the midst of the thicket. By spring the berries of the osoberry have already formed and hang in sparkling orange-red bunches among pale green leaves. The small pink blossoms of the brushy snowberry give off a sweet fragrance, particularly when wet with rain. Their large white berries hang on the bushes until late in winter.

Canary-yellow monkey-flowers line many of the moist ditches across the prairie, while purple iris prefer a dry area. Brilliant yellow Scotch broom invades much of western Washington, and flourishes in the stony ground in Thurston County. Its pungent odor fills the air until late spring.

Birds that make their summer home in western Washington begin arriving early in the spring. By May and June the western tanager sings from the tall firs, and the bright yellow warbler flits from bush to bush. Resident song sparrows render their lovely song again and again. Spring is the ideal time for this tour into the prairie land of southwestern Thurston County.

MILEAGE LOG

0.0   Go out park entrance road from picnic area parking lot of Millersylvania State Park and turn right on **State Route 121 (Tilley Road S.)**.

0.9   Turn right with S.R. 121 on **Maytown Road S.W.**

3.6   Go under I-5 and turn right at stop sign with Maytown Road toward Littlerock as S.R. 121 ends. Road shoulder, bicycle route signs.

6.5   Continue on **Littlerock Road S.W.** as it enters from the right at stop sign, then turn left with it one block farther. Public fishing access at mile 8.5.

13.9 Turn left on **U.S. 12** in Rochester. Grocery, drive-in, and coffee shop along U.S. 12.

15.0 Get into left-turn lane and turn left across railroad tracks on **183rd Avenue S.W.** Sheltered picnic table surrounded by green lawn, Masonic monument, historical monument marking the location of Fort Henness, and cemetery at mile 17.6.

18.7 Turn left on **Case Road S.W.** as 183rd Avenue heads up over I-5 overpass. Entrance to Scatter Creek Game Range on left at mile 20.3; pit toilets. *Note: Conservation license required to use game range facilities.* Watch for acute-angled rail crossing at mile 22.3. Cross Maytown Road S.W. at mile 24.5.

26.7 Turn right on **113th Avenue S.W.** as Case Road ends.

28.5 Turn right on **Tilley Road S.**

29.4 Turn right into entrance of Millersylvania State Park.

29.6 Picnic area parking lot; end of tour.

121 NISQUALLY–YELM–RAINIER

STARTING POINT: Parking lot of Nisqually National Wildlife Refuge. Take exit 114 (Nisqually) from I-5, turn north under I-5, and follow signs right to Nisqually National Wildlife Refuge.

DISTANCE: 43 miles.
TERRAIN: Moderate to flat.
TOTAL CUMULATIVE ELEVATION GAIN: 700 feet.
RECOMMENDED TIME OF YEAR: Any season.
RECOMMENDED STARTING TIME: 9 to 10 A.M.
ALLOW: 5 to 6 hours.
POINTS OF INTEREST
Medicine Creek Treaty monument in Old Nisqually
Centralia City Light Hydroelectric Plant

ELEVATION PROFILE

Much of the area covered in this tour is rich in historical background. The Medicine Creek Treaty, negotiated by Governor Isaac Stevens in 1854 as a covenant between the United States of America and the Indian tribes of Nisqually, Puyallup, and Squaxin, is commemorated by a monument in Old Nisqually. This small plaque on a boulder hardly seems fitting for a document that has caused such uproar over Indian fishing rights.

History of another sort is represented by the Centralia City Light Hydroelectric Plant, near Yelm. Although dwarfed by the hydroelectric facilities on the Columbia River, the three turbines of this power plant have supplied a major portion of Centralia's electricity since the plant's construction in 1928. A diversion dam several miles up the Nisqually River (see Tour 123) supplies water to the power canal feeding the penstocks. The plant's entrance road crosses an emergency spillway built to divert the canal's flow if an unplanned shutdown of the turbines occurs. Tours of the hydroelectric facility and the upstream diversion dam may be arranged by contacting the plant supervisor at least two days in advance. Write to Hydroelectic Plant Generation Manager, 14024 Yelm Highway S.E., Yelm, WA 98597; or call (206) 458-3901.

Dominating a major portion of this tour is the Fort Lewis Military Reservation. The fort was established as a training area at American Lake by the U.S. War Department in 1906. In 1917 the citizens of Pierce County donated real estate for the establishment of Camp Lewis. Enlarged over the years, the camp has become Fort Lewis, and has served as a base and training area for six wars. After many years of operation as an open fort, Fort Lewis was closed to the public in early 1987. Some of the training area remains open, but the main fort area requires military identification or special passes, arranged well in advance of entry.

MILEAGE LOG

0.0 Starting from the parking lot of the Nisqually National Wildlife Refuge, ride out the entrance road.

0.4 Turn left at stop sign, go under I-5, cross Martin Way S.E., and continue on **Nisqually Cutoff S.E.** as it bends left along the freeway. Dairy herds and truck garden crops cover the valley.

2.3 Turn left at a small wye on **7th Avenue S.E.** as Steilacoom Road S.E. goes right.

2.7 Turn right on **Old Pacific Highway S.E.** by Nisqually Valley Grocery as 7th Avenue ends. Monument to Medicine Creek Treaty here.

3.3 Turn left and steeply uphill on **Reservation Road S.E.** Cross bridge over main-line railroad tracks at mile 3.9.

6.3 Turn left on **State Route 510** as Reservation Road ends. Continue on paved shoulder.

6.6 Continue on S.R. 510 as Yelm Highway enters from the right at a wye. At mile 10.4 a dirt road leads left, by a sign announcing the Centralia City Light Hydroelectric Plant. *Note: This is a 0.9-mile side trip to penstock head gates and view of valley power plant. For a view, follow dirt path to the right just past diversion gates. Do not continue down to hydro plant unless appointment has been made for visit (see text). Return to S.R. 510 and continue south.* Enter Yelm at mile 11.7, where the road is named **Yelm Avenue W.** Food concessions at mile 12.5.

12.9 Cross railroad tracks and continue on **State Route 507** as it enters from the right and S.R. 510 ends. Restaurant, cafe, and grocery at mile 13.5.

14.0 Turn right on **Morris Road S.E.** as Creek Street goes left. Climb a short, steep hill.

15.8 Cross railroad tracks, turn right on **123rd Avenue S.E.**, and cross tracks again.

18.3 Turn left on **Koeppen Road S.E.** as 123rd Avenue ends.

19.5 Turn left on **State Route 507** as Koeppen Road ends. The highway has a rough, oiled shoulder. The road is named **Binghampton** as it enters Rainier.

21.1 Turn right on **Minnesota** toward East Olympia by Rainier Market & Deli and Albert's Drive-in. Cross railroad tracks, go under trestle, and start uphill as the road is renamed **Rainier Road S.E.** Continue right on Rainier Road as 138th Avenue S.E. goes left at mile 22.0. Cross Military Road S.E. at mile 23.3. Continue through prairie and forest of Fort Lewis Military Reservation, Rainier Training Area.

26.9 Turn right on **Spurgeon Creek Road S.E.** Extensive planting of strawberries appears as the road leaves the military area.

30.4 Turn right on **Yelm Highway S.E.** by country store.

31.8 Turn left on **Meridian Road S.E.** by gas-grocery.

32.5 Turn left on **58th Avenue S.E.**

33.5 Turn right on **Kagy Street S.E.**

34.0 Turn right at T junction on **Mullen Road S.E.**

34.2 Turn left on **Marvin Road S.E.** Cross two sets of railroad tracks.

Cross Pacific Avenue (State Route 510) at mile 37.1.

37.6 Turn right at traffic signal on **Steilacoom Road S.E.** Continue on shoulder marked Bicycle Lane, which ends at mile 38.8. Descend steep hill, cross McAllister Creek at bottom, and pass fish hatchery.

40.3 Bear left at wye with thoroughfare on **Nisqually Cutoff** as 7th Avenue S.E. goes on.

40.8 Cross Martin Way S.E. at stop sign, go under I-5, and turn right toward Nisqually National Wildlife Refuge.

42.6 End of tour in refuge parking lot.

*"Sorry, sir. You **must** have a gate pass."*

122 RAINIER–CLEAR LAKE

STARTING POINT: Town of Rainier. From the north take I-5 to exit 127 (State Route 512) toward Puyallup and Mt. Rainier. Turn right on State Route 7 toward Mt. Rainier and Tacoma and right again on State Route 507 to Rainier. From the south take exit 88A (Grand Mound) east to Tenino and follow State Route 507 to Rainier. Park in parking area on Dakota Street by Rainier City Hall, fire station, and school.

DISTANCE: 37 miles.
TERRAIN: Moderate.
TOTAL CUMULATIVE ELEVATION GAIN: 850 feet.
RECOMMENDED TIME OF YEAR: Clear Lake fishing access open mid-April to mid-July. Avoid opening weekend of lake fishing; otherwise, any season.
RECOMMENDED STARTING TIME: 9 to 10 A.M.
ALLOW: 5 hours.
POINTS OF INTEREST
Groves of oak and aspen trees
Camas lilies May through June

Snow began to fall, lightly at first, then more heavily, covering the countryside with a soft, white blanket. Our narrow bicycle tires bit through to the blacktop pavement. Muffled sounds seemed distant, yet close at hand. The twittering of the juncos and scolding of the winter wrens lost some of their usual intensity, and even the jets overhead could not disturb the peaceful solitude. Unconcerned by the falling snow, with their warm breath forming a misty fog, furry-coated horses stood calmly under huge, spreading oaks. The facial expressions of a power line crew, eating lunch in their big truck, showed utter disbelief that anyone would ride a bicycle in such weather. The old Clackamas schoolhouse and gymnasium, a relic of days gone by, stood empty and forlorn. Evening grosbeaks made cracking noises as they opened the seedpods still hanging on the bigleaf maple trees. Fences with closed gates surrounded the residential community of Clearwood; no one was looking at homesites on that snowy day.

A deserted, white field sloped from the road down to the shores of Clear Lake, marking the Department of Wildlife boat-launching ramp, but it was not exactly the time of year for a picnic by the lake. Snow began sticking to the roads and packing up under the bicycle fenders before our return to Rainier. A wintry day was a fascinating time for a tour of the backroads in Thurston County, but a ride need not be postponed for these conditions; this tour would be a different but pleasant scene in any other season.

MILEAGE LOG

0.0 Starting from parking area on Dakota Street in Rainier, head east, paralleling school grounds.

0.1 Turn right at stop sign on **Algyer Road**. Name changes to **148th Avenue S.E.** at mile 3.1 as Runyon Road S.E. goes right.

3.9 Turn left on **Martinson Road S.E.**, which after 0.5 mile bends right and becomes **143rd Avenue S.E.**

5.3 Turn left on **Vail Road S.E.** by Deschutes Grange Hall No. 222 as 143rd Avenue ends.

8.6 Turn right on **Bald Hill Road S.E.** Four Corners Grocery here has deli bar.

12.2 Bear left at wye with Bald Hill Road as Smith Prairie Road S.E. continues on. Grocery on left at mile 17.7.

18.4 Turn left into Clear Lake Public Fishing Access. Toilet facilities, ducks to feed, view of lake, lunch stop. *Note: Conservation license required.* Return along **Bald Hill Road**.

21.5 Turn left on **Longmire Road S.E.** as Bald Hill Road prepares to dive down a steep hill.

22.5 Bear right with **Neat Road S.E.** as Longmire turns to gravel and is marked Dead End. Glimpses of Deschutes River.

24.6 Turn left on **Lawrence Lake Road S.E.** as Smith Prairie Road goes on. Deschutes River rolls by on the left.

26.7 Turn left on **153 Avenue S.E.**

27.5 Turn left on **Lindsay Road S.E.** by fire station #22, "Wildbunch." *Note: Alternate lunch break at Lawrence Lake fishing access, 1.1 miles left on Pleasant Beach Road as Lindsay Road bends right at mile 28.5.*

29.0 Turn left on **Vail Road S.E.** Cross Deschutes River at mile 29.8.

31.7 Continue on **Vail Cutoff S.E.** as Vail Loop S.E. goes left. Cross Deschutes River and climb hill.

33.4 Bear right at stop sign with Vail Cutoff S.E. Olympic Pipeline Co. pump station at mile 34.9.

35.6 Turn right on shoulder of **State Route 507** as Vail Cutoff ends.

36.2 Turn right on **Minnesota Avenue** in Rainier and bear left on diagonal street toward school parking lot.

36.3 End of tour.

123 McKENNA–RAINIER

STARTING POINT: McKenna Elementary School at junction of State Route 702 with State Route 507 just north of McKenna. From the north take I-5 to exit 127 (State Route 512) toward Puyallup and Mt. Rainier; turn right on State Route 7 toward Rainier and Tacoma and right again on State Route 507 through Roy to McKenna. From the south take I-5 to exit 88A and head east to Tenino. Pick up State Route 507 and continue northeast to McKenna. Park in parking area at north end of school complex.

DISTANCE: 31 to 42 miles.
TERRAIN: Flat to moderate.
TOTAL CUMULATIVE ELEVATION GAIN: 700 to 1000 feet.
RECOMMENDED TIME OF YEAR: Any season.
RECOMMENDED STARTING TIME: 8 to 10 A.M.
ALLOW: 4 to 6 hours.
POINTS OF INTEREST
Centralia City Light Power Canal
  Headworks
Views of Mt. Rainier

This tour along relatively traffic-free roads of Thurston County lies due west of Mt. Rainier, with magnificent views of the mountain from every twist and turn. Glaciers covered with snow embrace the massif and give it a perpetual blanket of white. During the summer months, after the snow has melted from the rocks and steep cliffs, the two outer peaks of the seemingly three-peaked giant appear jagged and smeared with brown. Columbia Crest alone remains smooth and unblemished.

Immigrants to Washington Territory in the mid 1880s claimed the natural prairie lying between the Nisqually and Deschutes rivers southeast of Olympia for their homesteads. Later owners brought water from the Nisqually River for irrigation, to increase the production of crops on the stony but fertile soil. A canal dug along the hillside above the river extended across the prairie from two miles below the mouth of Ohop Creek all the way to Yelm. Competition from an expanding agriculture eventually altered the economics of this farming area, and the irrigation system was abandoned. Today only a few dairy farms and chicken ranches survive. Owners of homes and acreage make their living elsewhere, but small garden plots and pastures still produce bountifully when carefully watered and tended.

Centralia City Light Power Project, begun in 1928, still diverts water from the Nisqually River and sends it via a canal to a power-generating plant near Yelm. A visit to this diversion dam requires permission from the Centralia City Light Hydroelectric Plant manager, preferably at least two days in advance. Write to Hydro Plant Generation Manager, 14024 Yelm Highway S.E., Yelm, WA 98587, or call (206) 458-3901. Civil engineering buffs will find the facility fascinating. The Washington State Department of Fisheries requires the river to be maintained above a minimum flow, and thus the amount of water diverted into the canal varies from season to season. Control gates and spillway form one end of a steel-and-concrete basin. A double set of fish screens, mandated by the fisheries department in 1955, stretches across the head of the basin. Completely automated, the screens slowly move up and down in succession as a water spray washes leaves and debris into a gutter leading back to the river's main channel. The screens are expensive to replace and can be damaged if trash is allowed to build up against them and create a differential pressure. A backup hydraulic power supply system for operating the screens stands ready. Once a year the screens receive a thorough hand-scrubbing. Barn swallows find the concrete ledges around the basin to be ideal nesting sites. Happy chatter accompanies their continuous search for insects on the wing. Swooping low over the water, they skim the surface with an occasional splash. An osprey, or fish hawk, makes regular patrols, periodically plunging into the river to emerge with a fish clutched in its talons. Shaking the water from its feathers as it gains altitude, the hawk soon disappears over the trees. Great blue herons wait patiently along the bank of the river for itinerant fish. With a quick jab of a long sharp beak, the heron acquires a meal.

A boat-launching site maintained by the Washington State Department of Wildlife offers public access to picturesque Lake Lawrence. Canoeists paddle quietly along a bit of marshland of the mushroom-shaped lake, while fishermen move slowly about in their motorized boats. Water-skiers crisscross the lake, stirring up the water. Mt. Rainier rises above them all, casting a reflection on the sun-drenched scene.

Logging of the forested hillsides south of the Deschutes River continues to be important to the economy of the little town of Rainier. Once the site of a Weyerhaeuser Company town with rows of homes for employees, the old town of Vail is gone. Employees now commute to the remaining logging headquarters and rail transfer yard.

MILEAGE LOG

0.0 Parking lot of McKenna Elementary School by junction of State Route 702 with State Route 507. Head south on **S.R. 507** toward McKenna. Continue through McKenna, crossing Nisqually River into Thurston County at mile 0.5.

0.7 Cross Centralia Power Canal and turn left on **Vail Road S.E.** toward Lawrence Lake, Clear Lake, and airport. *Note: Cook Road goes left at mile 1.3 to Centralia City Light Power Canal Headworks; round trip 8.2 miles, 1.5 miles gravel road each way. See text for tour of headworks.*

1.6 Turn left on **Bald Hill Road** by grocery store.

5.1 Go straight at wye on **Smith Prairie Road S.E.** as Bald Hill Road swings left. Turn right immediately on **Lawrence Lake Road S.E.**

6.2 Turn right on **153rd Avenue S.E.**

7.0 Turn left on **Lindsay Road S.E.** by fire station #22, "Wildbunch." *Note: Optional side trip goes left at mile 8.0 on Pleasant Beach Road S.E. to public fishing access on Lawrence Lake, 2.2 miles round trip. Possible picnic lunch site; pit toilets.*

8.5 Turn left on **Vail Road S.E.** Cross Deschutes River at mile 9.2, and continue with thoroughfare as it is renamed **Vail Cutoff S.E.**

11.2 Turn left with **Vail Loop S.E.** as Vail Cutoff continues across bridge. Cross logging road and railroad tracks at mile 12.1. Site of previous town of Vail on right at mile 12.4. Cross railroad tracks and Deschutes River at mile 13.3.

14.7 Continue on **Vail Cutoff S.E.** as Vail Loop ends.

16.0 Turn right on **State Route 507** toward Tacoma. As it enters Rainier it is named **Binghampton Street**. Drive-in cafe in Rainier.

16.5 Turn left (north) on **Minnesota Street** toward East Olympia in Rainier. Cross one set of railroad tracks, go under a trestle, and climb hill. Road changes name to **Rainier Road S.E.**

17.4 Go straight on **138th Avenue S.E.** as Rainier Road swings right.

18.9 Turn right on **Military Road S.E.** as 138 Avenue ends. Road name changes to **123rd Avenue S.E.** at mile 20.6.

21.9 Turn left on **Fillman Road S.E.** as 123 Avenue is posted Dead End. The road makes two successive right turns and is renamed **118th Avenue S.E.** and **Manke Road S.E.**

24.3 Cross railroad tracks and State Route 507. Continue right with thoroughfare at wye on **Koeppen Road S.E.**

24.4 Turn left on **123rd Avenue S.E.** Watch for dangerous railroad crossing at mile 26.9. Road is renamed **Hannus Road S.E.** as it bends right and left through green irrigated fields.

28.5 Turn left on **Vail Road S.E.** Cross Bald Hill Road by grocery store at mile 29.6.

30.5 Turn right on **State Route 507** and cross the Nisqually River into Pierce County. Continue through McKenna.

31.2 McKenna Elementary School; end of tour.

LEWIS COUNTY

124 CENTRALIA–LINCOLN CREEK–OAKVILLE

STARTING POINT: Fort Borst Park in Centralia. Take I-5 to exit 82. Head west on Harrison Avenue, turn left at the second traffic light on Johnson Road, and then left into parking lot by Centralia Community Swimming Pool and Borst Raquetball Court across from Centralia Middle School.

DISTANCE: 50 miles.
TERRAIN: Moderate to flat.
TOTAL CUMULATIVE ELEVATION GAIN: 750 feet.
RECOMMENDED TIME OF YEAR: Mid-May best for camas; otherwise, any season.
RECOMMENDED STARTING TIME: 9 to 10 A.M.
ALLOW: 6 hours.
POINTS OF INTEREST
Fort Borst blockhouse
Chehalis Indian Reservation

ELEVATION PROFILE

DISTANCE IN MILES

The territory around Centralia was one of the earliest to be partitioned into private land claims in Washington State. Much of the farm and prairie land covered in this tour was settled under the Donation Land Claim Act of 1850, by which a married couple could stake a claim to 640 acres of land and a single person could claim 320 acres. Although the local Chehalis Indians continued to be friendly and took no part in skirmishes, the Indian Wars of 1855–56 interrupted the firming up of these claims as families took refuge at Fort Henness near Rochester. The blockhouse at Fort Borst Park was used as a secure granary to supply troops in the White and Puyallup valleys. Originally located at the junction of the Chehalis and Skookum-chuck rivers, the blockhouse was moved to its present location in 1923 and presented to the city of Centralia as a memorial to early-day settlers by a descendant of the original donation land claim owners, Mary Adeline and Joseph Borst. Only a granite monument marks the location of Fort Henness (see Tour 121).

The natural prairies and bottom lands along the Chehalis and Skookum-chuck rivers had already been spoken for when settlers began to locate along Lincoln Creek. Stands of huge virgin timber, felled and stacked in gigantic piles, burned for days and nights as the clearing job continued. The logging industry was yet to come, and the trees were only a nuisance.

Deer, bear, elk, grouse, and tremendous flocks of ducks and geese provided easy pickings for cougars, incoming settlers, and the coastal Indian residents. Fish were there for the catching in the many lakes, streams, and rivers.

Chances are still good for seeing a wild animal or two along the back-roads of this tour. Winter and early spring are the best times for sightings of

125

the elusive tundra swan or the ubiquitous mallard and striking pintail. The distant, very low hooting of a blue grouse lends an eerie quality to the woodland summits. Occasionally a red-shafted flicker or Harris woodpecker plays a staccato accompaniment on an old resonant snag, and swallows of many varieties fly and swoop over fields all summer. Flocks of goldfinches swarm over the fields in spring. The blue camas lily, once a staple in the diet of the Chehalis Indians, blooms profusely along the roads.

This bicycle tour nudges the mind to visions and sounds of the past with miles of traffic-free roads, then brings it up short and back to the present on the return to Fort Borst Park alongside noisy I-5.

MILEAGE LOG

0.0   Fort Borst Park, Centralia. Leave west entrance of park and proceed west through the junior high school parking lot past the tennis courts. Go around end of schoolyard fence next to tennis court, through gateway in second fence, and continue on **Mt. Vista Road**.

1.0   Turn right on **Eshom Road** past Centralia High School.

1.9   Turn left on **Galvin Road** and travel into the countryside past a large dairy farm. Cross Chehalis River at 2.6.

3.2   Follow left with the main thoroughfare in Galvin as the road is renamed **Lincoln Creek Road**. Continue along the valley for several miles. Houses, orchards, and farm buildings hug the hillside along the edge of the valley.

14.8   Turn right and uphill on **Manners Road** toward Independence as the valley of Lincoln Creek narrows to its end. Top a summit and coast down into Independence Creek Valley.

16.7   Turn left on **Garrard Creek Road**; cross Independence Creek and follow along its banks. Road at first is narrow and rough but widens as it climbs to a summit at mile 19.7. Descend into another valley and pass a small fire station. Enter Grays Harbor County at mile 23.5.

24.3   Keep right toward Oakville as sign points left to Brooklyn.

27.7   Turn right at stop sign, cross Chehalis River, and continue through the Chehalis Indian Reservation. Enter Oakville on **State Street**. City park at corner of State and Main streets at mile 29.6 is the nominal lunch stop. Grocery store, drive-in, and restaurant are left a few blocks along U.S. 12 (Pine Street).

29.6   Head east out of Oakville on **Main Street**. As it leaves town the road is renamed **E. Blockhouse Road**. Continue on **Elma-Gate Road** as Blockhouse turns right at mile 30.5.

30.9   Turn right on **Howanut Road**, which crosses the Black River at mile 31.6 and bends left. Chehalis Indian Reservation Tribal Center on the right at the top of a rise.

34.1   Turn left on **Anderson Road S.W.** This is the county line between Grays Harbor and Thurston counties.

35.0   Cross U.S. 12 and continue on Anderson. Endure 0.3 mile of gravel.

35.2   Turn right on **McCormick Road S.W.** as Anderson ends and enter Thurston County. Road bends left, then right, and becomes **175 Avenue S.W.**

36.2 Turn right at T junction on **Moon Road S.W.**

36.5 Turn left on **School Land Road S.W.** Black River rolls slowly along on the left.

38.6 Road bends right and becomes **Albany Street S.W.** Enter Rochester at mile 38.7 as **Littlerock Road S.W.** joins from the left. Cross U.S. 12 at 38.8; drive-in and grocery. Continue out of Rochester on **Albany Street**.

39.9 Bear left with thoroughfare on **James Road S.W.** as it joins from the right. Pass several dairy farms.

43.4 Join **Old 9 Highway S.W.**, bear right, then immediately turn left on **Tea Street S.W.** Cross railroad tracks and turn right on **Grand Mound Way S.W.** State of Washington Maple Lane School is on the right across railroad tracks and Old 9 Highway.

44.5 Turn right on **Old 99 Highway S.W.** as Grand Mound Way ends. Continue on Old 99 Highway as Old 9 comes in from the right at mile 44.8.

45.2 Turn right on **Oregon Trail Road S.W.** for a short diversion away from the traffic on Old 99 Highway.

45.6 Turn left at T junction on **Prather Road S.W.**

45.9 Turn right on **Old 99 Highway S.W.** by gas-grocery. Enter Lewis County at mile 46.4 as rough, oiled shoulders along this busy old concrete highway give way to smooth blacktop.

48.0 Turn left on **Horsley Avenue**.

48.1 Turn left on **Foron Road**.

48.2 Turn right on **Bennett Road** and follow it as it turns right at mile 48.6 and becomes **Van Wormer Street**.

49.1 Turn left through a cemetery. Turn right on **Johnson Road** on the other side. Continue south to Fort Borst Park.

50.2 End of tour at parking lot by raquetball court.

125 ADNA–ROCHESTER–CENTRALIA

STARTING POINT: Back Memorial Lewis County Park in Adna. Take I-5 to exit 77 (State Route 6). Turn west 4.5 miles to Adna, then right on Bunker Creek Road, right on Dieckman Road, and right again into park.

DISTANCE: 51 miles.
TERRAIN: Moderate to hilly.
TOTAL CUMULATIVE ELEVATION GAIN: 900 feet.
RECOMMENDED TIME OF YEAR: Any season.
RECOMMENDED STARTING TIME: 9:30 A.M.
ALLOW: 6 hours.
POINTS OF INTEREST
Fort Borst blockhouse
Claquato historic sign

ELEVATION PROFILE

DISTANCE IN MILES

Although claimed by U.S. settlers over a century ago, the valleys of Lewis County are still sparsely settled in comparison with the neighboring counties of Pierce and King to the north. The Donation Land Claim Act of 1850 and the Homestead Act of 1862 allowed early farmers to acquire land with minor capital outlay, provided that it be brought under cultivation. Names of the original settlers are reflected in street and place names.

Crops of corn, barley, and oats flourish in the bottom land along the Chehalis River. Fields of lush green grass provide summer grazing for the many dairy herds as well as pungent silage for winter. During the rainy season, low-lying areas flood as they did a century ago, receiving upland silt to add to soil fertility and providing wintering sites for flocks of ducks and occasional swans. Deer appear near edges of pastures but vanish into the forest as bicycles approach.

Virgin forest long ago gave way to the axes and saws of settlers and lumberjacks, who cleared the valleys and denuded the hills. Rivers provided the original transportation arteries, but as farming and lumbering moved inland, railroads made their way up the valleys. In Lincoln Creek Valley remnants of the railroad, which operated into the 1930s, still protrude from creekbanks. As the roads were poor or nonexistent, railroads became the sole means of transportation. Household goods, supplies, and crops were moved by handcar along the rails, and children walked to and from school along the tracks. Eventually the trees were all cut and many of the railroads abandoned. Roads were built and gradually improved. All of the rural roads now are paved, providing delightful bicycle routes.

As the bicyclist of today climbs the summit of Michigan Hill and gazes eastward, Mt. Rainier presents its everlasting snow-covered and glaciated face as it did to the settler of yesteryear. Peaceful rural farmlands, pleasant forest settings, and expansive mountain vistas guarantee an enjoyable bicycle tour.

MILEAGE LOG

0.0 Turn left on **Dieckman Road** from Back Memorial Park entrance.

0.2 Turn right at stop sign and continue out of town on **Bunker Creek Road** and into valley farmland.

10.0 Turn right on **Ingalls Road** as Bunker Creek Road goes left to a dead end. Route climbs out of the valley, topping a summit at mile 11.0.

12.3 Cross Lincoln Creek and turn left on **Lincoln Creek Road**. Small single-engine fire station at mile 13.0.

13.8 Turn right on **Manners Road** and climb over a hill.

15.6 Keep right with **Independence Road S.W.** toward Rochester as Garrard Creek Road goes left to Oakville. Cross Independence Creek at mile 15.9. Pedal into rolling farmland, entering Thurston County at mile 16.3. Cross abandoned railroad grade at 20.3 and ride along the Chehalis River.

22.0 Continue on thoroughfare as Michigan Hill Road goes right under abandoned railroad trestle. Cross the Chehalis River. *Note: Route returns to this point after lunch stop in Rochester.*

22.9 Turn left on **Marble Street S.W.**, which bends right and becomes **185th Avenue S.W.**

23.8 Turn left on **Albany Street S.W.** by Swede Hall.

24.1 Junction with U.S. 12 in Rochester city center. Grocery and coffee shop on right, drive-in cafe on left. After lunch return along route and across the Chehalis River.

26.3 Turn left on **Michigan Hill Road S.W.**, duck under a low railroad trestle, then turn left on **Lundeen Road S.W.** and start climbing a steep hill. Views of Chehalis Valley at mile 27.3.

30.0 Turn left on **Prather Road S.W.** as Lundeen Road ends. Begin a gradual, then steep descent. Cross abandoned railroad grade and the Chehalis River at 32.2.

33.6 Turn right on **Old 99 Highway S.W.** at stop sign by gas-grocery. Reenter Lewis County at mile 34.1 as a wide, paved shoulder begins.

35.5 Turn right on **Sandra Avenue**.

36.2 Turn right on **Galvin Road**, then left on **Eshom Road**.

36.8 Turn left on **Borst Avenue**.

37.8 Turn right on **Belmont Avenue** at entrance to Fort Borst Park. Make a stop at the rest rooms as necessary and continue around the traffic circle past the Fort Borst blockhouse.

38.0 Exit through park gate and take sidewalk right toward I-5 underpass and continue right on **Harrison Avenue**. A ramped sidewalk is available here, leading to a marked bicycle lane.

38.9 Bear left with thoroughfare on **W. Main** and immediately turn right on **Yew Street**.

39.4 Turn right on **Mellen Street** and again go under the freeway. Cross the Chehalis River at mile 39.8.

39.9 Turn left on **Military Road**.

40.6 Make another left turn on **Scheuber Road** as it heads into the countryside. Views of Mt. Rainier and Mt. St. Helens.

45.4 Turn right on **State Route 6** as Scheuber Road comes to an end. Interesting historical sign at Claquato at 45.6.

45.7 Turn left on **Highway 603** by grocery and cross the Chehalis River.

46.4 Turn right on **Twin Oaks Road**. Although the original oaks are gone, two sets of twin oaks remain to justify the name.

50.0 Turn right on **State Route 6** and cross the Chehalis River.

50.3 Turn left on **Bunker Creek Road** and enter Adna. Grocery store on the left.

50.5 Turn right on **Dieckman Road**.

50.7 Turn right into Back Memorial Park; end of tour.

126 HANAFORD VALLEY

STARTING POINT: Fort Borst Park in Centralia. Take I-5 to exit 82. Head west on Harrison Avenue, turn left at the second traffic light on Johnson Road, and then left into parking lot by swimming pool and Fort Borst Raquetball Court across from Centralia Middle School.

DISTANCE: 38 miles.
TERRAIN: Some hilly, some flat.
TOTAL CUMULATIVE ELEVATION GAIN: 1050 feet.
RECOMMENDED TIME OF YEAR: May is recommended for spring flowers.
RECOMMENDED STARTING TIME: 9:30 A.M.
ALLOW: 5 hours plus time for optional steam plant tour.
POINT OF INTEREST
Centralia Steam Electric Project

ELEVATION PROFILE

[Elevation profile chart showing elevation in feet (0', 200', 400', 600') versus distance in miles (0, 10, 20, 30, 40), with labels STEAM PLANT and BUCODA marked by arrows near miles 20 and 30.]

DISTANCE IN MILES

The botanist, the bird watcher, and the electric power engineer all will find features of interest in this tour. In spring the wild blue camas lily, a native of the Chehalis Valley, provides large masses of color. Its onionlike bulb was an important food to the coastal Indians, and camas fields were tribal property guarded against trespassers. The lavender, tough-leaved wild iris decorates the roadside along cuts and fills. Serviceberry bushes, some growing to a height of 15 feet, add clouds of white blossoms to the scene. The white plumes of the false Solomon's seal and the delicate twin white bells of the Oregon fairy bells arch from the banks along the road. Later, berries replace the blossoms. In the Hanaford Valley, virtually pure stands of timber-sized Oregon ash trees (a hardwood forest is unusual in western Washington), plus common inhabitants of the montane forest, such as sword fern and bleeding heart, make this tour a botanist's delight.

The roadside terrain, ranging from valley to prairie to forest, offers opportunities for seeing and hearing a wide variety of birds. The savannah sparrow and the goldfinch share the prairie with the robin, meadowlark, swallow, and red-shafted flicker. Buteo hawks soar the thermals along the hillsides. In the forest, the winter wren spews out his high-pitched, rapid-fire aria. Vireos, kinglets, and warblers stay high in the trees, their distinctive

songs revealing their presence. Add to this the display of exotic pheasants at the game farm close to the starting point, and you have a tour for birders.

As the bicyclist rounds a bend in the Hanaford Valley, Mt. Rainier shows its three peaks, then the Centralia Steam Electric Plant with its two tall smokestacks comes into view. On the right, four banks of evaporative cooling towers send billows of fog shooting into the air. Alongside the plant a large blue rectangular lake forms a surge reservoir for cooling water. Entrance to the green lawns and parking lot beside the visitor center is through a guarded fence. Guided plant tours, available July through March, must be arranged beforehand by contacting the plant supervisor, Route 2, Box 42, Centralia, WA 98531. At the visitor center interesting pictorial displays explain coal mining, power production, and ecological restoration projects.

The Centralia Steam Electric Project went on-line in 1971, culminating more than a decade of planning and development by the electric-power industry of the Pacific Northwest. Large low-sulfur soft coal reserves that provide the fuel for this plant are mined by economical surface methods, and the land is rehabilitated to productive uses as the mining progresses.

Next to the plant a giant machine gnaws at huge piles of coal, reminding one of a big gold-mining dredge as it sits between the morainelike coal piles, swinging its huge bucket-toothed wheel, gulping up coal, and sending it to the furnace via a network of covered, inclined beltways. A road overpass allows enormous trucks to haul the coal from the mine to the processing plant.

Views of the open-pit mine areas from the hill roads east of the old town site of Tono are impressive: whole mountains have been gnawed away. A brisk dash down the final hill is followed by a crossing of the Skookumchuck River at the edge of the historic town of Bucoda, the site of the first territorial prison, whose inmates worked in the adjacent coal mine.

Traffic picks up on State Route 507 as the route winds through Waunch Prairie and follows the Skookumchuck River back to Centralia.

MILEAGE LOG

0.0 Fort Borst Park in Centralia. Leave the west entrance of the park; proceed through the junior high school parking lot past tennis courts. Go around end of schoolyard fence next to tennis court, go through gateway in second fence, and continue on **Mt. Vista Road**. Lewis County Game Farm displays pens of pheasants. Road bends right by Centralia High School and is renamed **Eshom Road**.

1.6 Turn left on **Galvin Road** as Eshom ends, and proceed past dairy farms. Cross Chehalis River at mile 2.6.

3.1 Turn left on **Joppish Road** in Galvin and proceed out of town. Enjoy the flora and fauna as this delightful traffic-free road leaves the valley and winds through the forested hillside to upland pastures.

4.9 Turn left on **Cooks Hill Road** as Joppish Road ends at the summit of the hill. Descend hill and enter Centralia on a broad, concrete road. Pass Centralia General Hospital and continue under I-5, where the road name changes to **Mellen Street (State Route 507)**. Follow

S.R. 507 as it is marked **Alder Street** and **S. Cherry Street** in succession.

8.7 Turn right on **S. Silver Street** as a traffic light appears one block ahead on Cherry.

9.1 Turn left on **Summa Street**, cross railroad tracks and both one-way lanes of State Route 507, and head out into an open green valley, where the road is renamed **E. Summa Street** and finally **Salzer Valley Road**.

12.9 Bear left with main thoroughfare as Reinke Road (dead end) goes on. Climb a short, gentle hill, then tackle a longer, steeper one.

15.0 Don't miss this left turn on **Little Hanaford Road** as L. Hanaford Road continues on. Go past a dip in the road and immediately turn right on **Teitzel Road**, which shortly emerges into the valley of South Hanaford Creek.

16.7 Turn left with Teitzel Road as Teitzel Road E. goes right.

19.5 Turn right on **Big Hanaford Road**. Mt. Rainier visible at the end of the valley. Soon the twin smokestacks of the Centralia Steam Electric Plant come into view.

21.4 Turn left into steam plant's main office entrance drive. *Note: If a guided tour has been arranged, report to the security gate.* Permission should be requested for a short snack break on the front steps or lawn. Return out the entrance gate and continue left on Big Hanaford Road past the power plant and coal piles.

24.4 Turn left on **Tono Road S.E.** after crossing Hanaford Creek. The road traverses two summits with a creek valley between. As the road descends from the second summit, the gigantic excavation of the open-pit coal mine comes into view. Bucoda Volunteer Park appears on the left just before the road crosses the Skookumchuck River. Park has tables and a shelter. Children swim in the placid river by the park. Cross bridge and enter Bucoda on **7th Street**.

28.4 Turn right on **Main Street**. Tavern, grocery, and post office. Turn left on **6th Street**, then left on **State Route 507** toward Centralia. Cross Skookumchuck River at 32.3 as Waunch Prairie broadens out. Enter Lewis County at 33.0.

33.8 Bear right with highway and cross the Skookumchuck River as Hanaford Road goes left to the steam plant. Lewis County Schafer Park on east bank of the river. Enter Centralia on **Downing Street**, which bends left by grocery and becomes **N. Pearl Street**.

35.7 Turn right on **Reynolds Avenue** shortly before Pearl Street crosses railroad tracks and steel bridge over the Skookumchuck. Cross railroad tracks under I-5 viaduct at mile 36.7. Bear left and right with Reynolds over more tracks at 36.9.

37.1 Turn left on **Johnson Road**. Cross Harrison Avenue at light at 37.5.

37.8 Back at parking lot in Fort Borst Park.

127 CENTRALIA–CHEHALIS

STARTING POINT: Fort Borst Park in Centralia. Take I-5 to exit 82. Turn west on Harrison Avenue, left at the second traffic light on Johnson Road, and then left into parking lot by Centralia Community Swimming Pool and Borst Raquetball Court across from Centralia Middle School.

DISTANCE: 24 miles.
TERRAIN: Mostly flat (two hills).
TOTAL CUMULATIVE ELEVATION GAIN: 600 feet.
RECOMMENDED TIME OF YEAR: Any season. Roads may be under water during spring floods.
RECOMMENDED STARTING TIME: 9 A.M. to 2 P.M.
ALLOW: 3 to 4 hours.
POINTS OF INTEREST
Claquato Cemetery
Claquato Church

ELEVATION PROFILE

This 24-mile loop tour between Centralia and Chehalis follows the back-roads of the Chehalis River Valley west of I-5. A climb to the summit of Cook Hill near the start of the ride gives the bicyclist a short workout. When joined with Millersylvania–Centralia (Tour 51), Morton–Millersylvania (Tour 50), Chehalis–Lewis and Clark State Park (Tour 128), or Rainbow Falls–Sea-quest (Tour 132), this tour provides a vital link in north-south backroad bicycle routes of western Washington State.

Dairy and beef cattle graze the pastures near the Chehalis River as the route leaves Centralia and touches the southeastern tip of the valley of Lincoln Creek. Leaving the valley, the route climbs the forested hillside to upland pastures before plunging back downhill into the outskirts of Centralia and heading south. Mt. St. Helens, with its abruptly truncated volcanic cone, appears on the southeastern horizon. Views into the history of early Lewis County are offered by a side trip up the Claquato Cemetery hill.

West Side Park, a short diversion across I-5 in Chehalis, provides a pleasant spot for the summer picnic lunch. For cold-weather bicycle tour-ists, restaurants in downtown Chehalis are easily reached by continuing past the park on N.W. West Street, or alternatively continuing on the route to the golf course cafe by the airport. The fragrant aroma of peppermint announces the closeness of the Chehalis industrial district; the I. P. Callison and Sons plant is a major processor of peppermint oil, extracting the flavoring from freshly mowed peppermint leaves brought by the truckload over the Cascades from the Yakima Valley.

Numerous oxbow lakes along the airport road attract several varieties of ducks, while the osprey, or fish hawk, occasionally dives in to garner his share of the aquatic population.

Always interesting and often provocative, the Hamilton Farms signboard to the right of Airport Road near I-5 signals the return to Centralia and the end of an enjoyable bicycle tour.

MILEAGE LOG

0.0 Parking lot by Centralia Community Pool. Turn left at parking lot exit, then immediately right through the junior high school parking lot past tennis courts. Circumvent end of schoolyard fence next to tennis court, go through gateway in second fence, and continue on **Mt. Vista Road**. Lewis County Game Farm displays pens of pheasants.

1.0 Turn right on **Eshom Road** past Centralia High School.

1.7 Turn left on **Galvin Road** and pass a dairy farm. Cross Chehalis River at mile 2.6.

3.2 Turn left on **Lincoln Creek Road** in Galvin as Galvin Road ends.

3.9 Turn left on **Cooks Hill Road**. Enjoy the flora and fauna as this delightful traffic-free road leaves the valley and climbs to upland pastures and a summit at mile 5.6.

6.0 Pass a fire station and turn right on **Blanchard Road**. **Graf Road** joins from the right at mile 7.6.

7.9 Bear right with Graf Road as Scammon Creek Road goes left.

8.4 Turn right on **Scheuber Road** as it heads into the countryside. Views of Mt. Rainier to the northeast and Mt. St. Helens on the southeastern horizon.

13.1 Turn right on **State Route 6** as Scheuber Road comes to an end. Interesting historical sign about Claquato at 13.3. *Note: A 0.5-mile side trip leads uphill on Stearns Road to Claquato Cemetery, down Water Street past historic church with bronze bell, to S.R. 6.*

13.4 Turn left on **Highway 603** and cross Chehalis River. Cross two sets of railroad tracks before heading up a very steep hill. Top a summit at mile 14.5.

14.6 Turn left on **Tune Road** and plunge downhill.

16.3 Turn left on **Shorey Road**. Cross Newaukum River and more railroad tracks at mile 16.5, where the road is renamed **S.W. Newaukum Avenue**. Cross State Route 6 at mile 17.2 and continue on **N.W. Louisiana Avenue**.

17.8 Turn left on **N.W. Airport Road** as N.W. West Street goes right over I-5 to West Side Park and downtown Chehalis. Riverside Golf Course at mile 18.4 has a small cafe. Several oxbow ponds attract ducks and osprey at 20.3. Hamilton Farm signboard is on right along I-5.

21.8 Turn right at a stop sign on **Mellen Street (State Route 507)**; go under I-5 and into Centralia.

22.1 Turn left on **Yew Street**.

22.7 Turn left on **W. Main Street**, then immediately bear right as thoroughfare changes name to **Harrison Avenue**.

23.5 Get up on the sidewalk, go under I-5, and cross Harrison Avenue with traffic light. After crossing, get up on sidewalk and bear right on **Borst Avenue** past entrance to Fort Borst Park.

23.8 Turn left on **Johnson Road** at stop sign.

23.9 Turn left into parking lot by Centralia Community Pool; end of ride.

128 CHEHALIS–LEWIS AND CLARK STATE PARK (Newaukum Valley)

STARTING POINT: Angle parking along north side of Recreation Park in Chehalis. Take exit 76 from I-5; proceed east 0.5 mile on Parkland Drive and S.W. 13th Street. Turn left on William Avenue to parking area. Additional parking available at Stan Hedwal Park, 0.6 mile along route.

DISTANCE: 36 miles.
TERRAIN: Easy to moderate.
TOTAL CUMULATIVE ELEVATION GAIN: 750 feet.
RECOMMENDED TIME OF YEAR: Any season.
RECOMMENDED STARTING TIME: 9 A.M. to 2 P.M.
ALLOW: 4 hours.
POINTS OF INTEREST
Chehalis Recreation Park
Jackson Prairie School
Jackson Courthouse Historic Site
Lewis and Clark State Park

ELEVATION PROFILE

Lewis County dates back to 1845, when the area lying north of the Columbia River to latitude 54° 40' and west of the Cowlitz River to the Pacific Ocean was designated as separate from Vancouver County. All of this happened before the Oregon Territory was created in 1848 and before the boundary between the United States and Canada had been finalized. By the time Washington Territory became a fact of life in 1853, Pacific, Thurston, King, Pierce, Jefferson, and Island counties had been carved from Lewis County. The remaining counties west of the Cascade Mountains evolved from these, and all were in existence by the time Washington entered the union in 1889. Chehalis has been the Lewis County seat since 1872, when the honor was snatched away from the declining little town of Claquato. The Northern Pacific Railroad's decision to lay tracks through Chehalis helped to swing the decision.

Today, Claquato is marked by a historical sign along State Route 6, while Chehalis is a modern, thriving city. The residents of Chehalis are proud of its history and display the McKinley Stump, which was cut near Pe Ell in 1901, boasts a pagoda roof, and was erected for President William McKinley's reception that year. President Theodore Roosevelt spoke from this stump in 1903. The production of lumber is still an important industry for Chehalis.

This tour also touches another famous landmark. The Jackson Courthouse near U.S. 12 at Mary's Corner is the oldest standing building used for courthouse purposes in the State of Washington. It was built as a private home in 1850 and became an important stopping place for travelers in Washington Territory.

History of a different sort is evident at the Lewis and Clark State Park. Columbus Day 1962 brought a storm of hurricane proportions to the State of Washington. Many big trees were toppled in the high winds, and the camping area in this state park was devastated. A young Douglas fir forest now surrounds the rebuilt campground. Amazingly enough, the big trees along the extensive nature trail in the park were not blown over and present an informative two- to three-mile hike.

MILEAGE LOG

0.0 Starting from the north side of Recreation Park on **William Avenue**, head east and turn right on **S.W. 13th Street**. Follow thoroughfare as it bends right and is renamed **S.W. Parkland Drive**.

0.5 Cross I-5 on overpass and ride out into farmland along the Newaukum River. Chehalis's Stan Hedwall Park at mile 0.6 has camping, picnic shelters, and playground. Road name changes to **Rice Road**.

3.0 Turn left on **LaBree Road** as Rice Road ends.

3.4 Turn right on **Hamilton Road** as LaBree Road turns left.

4.8 Turn right with Hamilton Road as Hamilton Road North goes left.

5.5 Turn left under freeway on **Rush Road**, and immediately turn right on

Kirkland Road. Cross Newaukum River at mile 6.0.

8.1   Turn left on **Forest Napavine Road E.** as Kirkland Road ends.

9.3   Turn right on **Jackson Highway**. Lewis County Road Department Central Shop is on the right. Good five-foot-wide paved shoulders. Cross State Route 508 at mile 10.8 and proceed up moderate grade. Jackson Prairie School, built in early 1900s, now houses an antique shop on the right at 12.8. Matilda Jackson Roadside Park on right at mile 13.1; picnic shelter with tables surrounded by many large fir trees. *Note: Tour may be shortened by 4.5 miles by turning right on Avery Road at mile 13.2.*

13.3   Cross U.S. 12 at Mary's Corner. Jackson Courthouse Historic Site

141

just beyond on the left. Old-growth tree exhibit on the right at mile 14.5.

15.1 Turn right into Lewis and Clark State Park; picnic area with shelters, camping sites, and nature trail. Allow 0.5 mile for bicycling around the park.

15.6 Leave park entrance and turn right on Jackson Highway.

15.9 Turn right on **Park Road** as Oyler Road goes left. Cross I-5 on an overpass at mile 19.0.

19.5 Turn right on **N. Military Road**. *Note: Mustard Seed Cafe is right 0.4 mile on Avery Road W. at four-way stop at mile 22.0.*

23.0 Turn left on **Koontz Road** as Military Road ends. As it enters Napavine, the road is renamed **E. Washington Street**.

24.4 Turn right on **2nd Avenue N.E.** in Napavine by grocery, cafe, and bakery. Mayme Shaddock Park on left at 24.4. Second Avenue becomes **Rush Road** as it leaves Napavine and descends a long hill.

26.2 Turn left on **Newaukum Valley Road** just before Rush Road crosses the Newaukum River. Road traverses the hillside along the edge of the valley, providing nice views of the farms.

28.8 Turn left and uphill on **Rogers Road**. Cross Burlington Northern main-line tracks at mile 29.6 and continue up a short, steep hill.

29.9 Turn right on **Shorey Road** and coast downhill. Shorey Road becomes **S.W. Newaukum Avenue** just after crossing the Newaukum River at mile 32. *Note: To shorten tour by 0.5 mile, turn right on sidewalk under I-5 to Main Street at mile 32.8.* Cross State Route 6 at mile 32.9 and continue on **N.W. Louisiana Avenue**.

33.5 Turn right on **N.W. West Street** as N.W. Airport Road goes left, and cross I-5 on overpass.

33.9 Turn right on **N.W. State Avenue** just past first set of railroad tracks.

34.2 Turn left on **W. Main Street**.

34.4 Turn right on **S.W. Chehalis Avenue**. Road bends left at mile 35.2 and becomes **S.W. 9th Street**.

35.3 Turn right on **S.W. Pacific Avenue** as 9th Street crosses railroad tracks.

35.4 Turn left on **S.W. 11th Street** at stop sign, cross railroad tracks, and turn right on **S.W. William Avenue**. End of tour at mile 35.5.

129 LEWIS AND CLARK STATE PARK– ONALASKA

STARTING POINT: Lewis and Clark State Park. Take exit 68 from I-5, then U.S. 12 east 2.7 miles to Mary's Corner. Turn right (south) on Jackson Highway and proceed 1.6 miles to the park entrance. Park in the picnic area parking lot.

DISTANCE: 45 miles.
TERRAIN: Some hilly, some flat.
TOTAL CUMULATIVE ELEVATION GAIN: 1450 feet.
RECOMMENDED TIME OF YEAR: Any season. September through November best for salmon hatchery tour, last Sunday in August for Steam Threshing Bee.
RECOMMENDED STARTING TIME: 9 to 10 A.M.
ALLOW: 6 to 8 hours.
POINTS OF INTEREST
Lewis and Clark State Park
Jackson Courthouse Historic Site
Cowlitz Salmon Hatchery
Cowlitz Trout Hatchery
Cowlitz Mission

ELEVATION PROFILE
DISTANCE IN MILES

During the years in which the Hudson's Bay Company traded in the Pacific Northwest, it operated a farming subsidiary called the Puget Sound Agricultural Company. Some of the most productive land was the natural prairie north of the Cowlitz River near Toledo in Lewis County. Although the Cowlitz Prairie is no longer a major producer of hay and grains, it still offers the wide horizons of an open prairie, cultivated by "gentleman farmers" and grazed by a few dairy farms. Also an important part of the area's history is the St. Francis Xavier (Cowlitz) Mission, which staked one of the early donation land claims on the prairie. Founded in 1838, the mission is the oldest in the Northwest and the first Catholic Church in what was to become Washington State. The nearby cemetery provides another link to the past.

To attend the Steam Threshing Bee, held the last Sunday in August at the Robert Herren Ranch on the prairie, is to step back in time. Steam-engine buffs come hundreds of miles to operate and exhibit their steam tractors. Coupled to threshers by long, twisted, flat belts, the big wood-burning engines make quick work of piles of wheat sheaves. Other steam tractors roll over the pastureland, entertaining the crowds with their shrill whistles and distinctive chuffing and hissing sounds. A steam tractor also powers a buzz saw to cut wood for the boilers.

This tour also explores the valleys of the Newaukum and Cowlitz rivers and the ridges separating them. These two rivers produced a bountiful supply of fish for early settlers. The Cowlitz River was one of the major sources of salmon and trout. When Tacoma City Light planned its huge hydroelectric project on the Cowlitz, it put as much planning and money into

143

protecting and producing fish as into equipment for generating electricity. The Cowlitz Salmon Hatchery, now operated by the Washington State Department of Fisheries, is the world's largest. The trout hatchery raises and releases thousands of steelhead, sea-run cutthroat, and rainbow trout into the Cowlitz River. Visits to these facilities top off this vigorous and scenic bicycle tour.

MILEAGE LOG

0.0   Picnic area parking lot, Lewis and Clark State Park. Follow park road to exit and turn left on **Jackson Highway**. Jackson Courthouse Historic Site on right at mile 1.7. Cross U.S. 12 at mile 1.8; Matilda Jackson Roadside Park on left 0.4 mile farther. Head downhill and cross State Route 508 at mile 4.3.

5.4   Turn right on **Middle Fork Road** and cross South Fork Newaukum River at 5.8.

6.1   Turn left on **Rosebrook Road**. North Fork Newaukum appears on right as road bends left.

7.6   Turn right on **North Fork Road** as Rosebrook ends. Cross the North Fork Newaukum River on a one-lane bridge and enter a lovely wide valley. Although frequently bathed in clouds and fog, Mt. Rainier sometimes looms over the greensward.

11.2   Turn right on **Centralia Alpha Road** and cross North Fork Newaukum River. Start up a long hill through dense second-growth forest of alder and fir. Top a summit at mile 13.0, dive downhill, cross a creek, and climb to a second summit, where the road levels out.

15.0   Turn right on **Beck Road**.

16.3   Turn right on **Middle Fork Road** as Beck Road ends.

17.2   Turn left on **Deggler Road** toward Onalaska. Plunge downhill and into a broad, open valley. A tall smokestack marks the location of an old lumber mill as Mt. St. Helens comes into view on the southern horizon. Road name changes to **Carlisle Avenue** as it enters Onalaska. A small park is on the left by the high school; a diminutive drive-in on the right. Cross State Route 508 at mile 18.9 and continue on **Leonard Road;** grocery and cafe on left. Cross South Fork Newaukum River at 19.2.

19.8   Turn left on **Burchett Road** and proceed uphill past small farms and woodlots.

22.3   Turn right on **Fred Plant Road** at bottom of a downhill grade.

23.5   Turn left on **Gore Road** as Fred Plant Road ends. Road winds through hay fields before heading down a short, steep hill.

25.6   Turn right on **Stowell Road** as Gore Road ends, and enter Salkum.

25.9   Turn right on **Salkum Road**; Salkum Drive-in at mile 26. Cross U.S. 12 at mile 26.1 and continue through pastureland on **Fuller Road** as it descends toward the river. Small grocery on the left at mile 27.0.

27.3   Turn left on **Spencer Road** as Fuller Road ends on a cliff overlooking the Cowlitz River. Descend 0.7 mile to the Cowlitz Salmon Hatchery for a self-guided tour. After touring the hatchery, return to Spencer Road and proceed along the high bluff above the Cowlitz River. Long strings of pale green lichen (*Usnea longissima*), some eight to ten feet long, decorate the trees.

33.9   Turn left 0.3 mile for the Cowlitz Trout Hatchery and Visitor Center, hours 8 A.M. to 5 P.M. Tour the hatchery and landscaped visitor center, then return to Spencer Road.

34.5   Turn left and continue uphill on **Spencer Road**. The road dips into a small creek valley and emerges on the broad, cultivated Cowlitz

Prairie. The horizon broadens to the Olympic Mountains in the west, Mt. Rainier in the east, and Mt. St. Helens in the south. At mile 39.0 pass the Robert Herren Ranch, location of the annual Steam Threshing Bee. The Cowlitz Mission sits atop a hill at mile 39.8. St. Mary's Center shares the panoramic site.

40.1 Turn right on **Jackson Highway**. Pass the Toledo-Winlock Airport at mile 40.7.

43.9 Turn left into Lewis and Clark State Park. Follow park road traffic pattern past the rest rooms to the picnic area parking lot. End of ride at mile 44.3.

"It's called Usnea longissima, *Charlie . . . Charlie?"*

130 ADNA–LEWIS AND CLARK STATE PARK

STARTING POINT: Back Memorial Lewis County Park in Adna. Take I-5 to exit 77 (State Route 6). Turn west, proceed 4.5 miles to Adna, turn right on Bunker Creek Road, right on Dieckman Road, then right again into park. Gate is locked at 8 P.M.

DISTANCE: 48 miles.
TERRAIN: Half hilly, half flat; 5 miles of steep gravel road.
TOTAL CUMULATIVE ELEVATION GAIN: 2000 feet.
RECOMMENDED TIME OF YEAR: August through October for best condition of gravel road.
RECOMMENDED STARTING TIME: 8:00 to 9:30 A.M.
ALLOW: 5 to 7 hours.
POINTS OF INTEREST
Winolequa Park, Winlock
St. Urban Church
Lewis and Clark State Park
Jackson Courthouse Historic Site

This 48-mile tour in Lewis County covers many different types of terrain, giving the bicyclist a chance to observe and experience several changes of scenery. After a very short stretch of the Chehalis Valley, the route heads steeply up the hill toward Curtis. Acres of neatly sheared Christmas trees cover much of the countryside, while young Douglas fir forests cling to the steeper slopes and give promise of continued timber harvests in years to come. Oak and ash trees mingle with alder, willow, fir, and maple as the route follows the valley along Lake Creek. Several old homesteads, long abandoned, nestle among vines and shrubs that almost engulf them. Other old homes present a picture of continued interest and intensive care.

The route follows a steep gravel road as it traverses the ridge northwest of Winlock and winds uphill through dense second-growth forest of fir and cedar. Pavement again covers the road surface as habitations lay claim to isolated clearings.

Grassy fields, ringed with fir and cedar trees, identify Grand Prairie east of Winlock. A short side trip leads to Winlock's delightful Winolequa Park, which derives the latter half of its name from adjacent Olequa Creek. A large, well-equipped kitchen shelter serves the many picnic tables scattered among the trees. After a short meander along the rolling plateau, the route dips to the valley again, where thick stands of Oregon ash, oak, and aspen trees present an unusual display of deciduous hardwood forest. A two- to three-mile nature trail in Lewis and Clark State Park offers an opportunity to view virgin fir and cedar trees and to identify many other lowland flora such as devil's club, hazelnut, vine maple, and the unusual inside-out flower. As the tour climbs to the plateau again and continues across Jackson Prairie, gladioli thrive in nurseries, presenting a colorful display during summer.

Fields of wheat, oats, corn, and grass cover the fertile mouth of Pleasant Valley all summer long. Sprinkler irrigation systems provide added moisture to ensure a bountiful harvest. Peas are an important early crop.

Varied scenery, low-traffic roads, and occasional views of both Mt. Rainier and Mt. St. Helens add crowning touches to an enjoyable bicycle tour.

MILEAGE LOG

0.0 Back Memorial Park parking lot. Go out entrance road and turn left on **Dieckman Road**.

0.3 Turn left on **Bunker Creek Road**.

0.5 Turn right on **State Route 6** and cross the Chehalis River. Grocery. Watch for acute-angled railroad tracks at mile 1.0.

1.6 Turn left on **Curtis Hill Road**. Proceed steeply uphill past several homes. Huge old English walnut trees hang over fences near the summit at mile 3.3. Plunge downhill past a Weyerhaeuser clearcut (winter 1976–77) that has been replanted to Douglas fir trees.

4.9 Turn left on **Lake Creek Road**. Downtown Curtis, 0.1 mile farther on Curtis Hill Road, consists of a store, service station, and post office all in one building.

6.0 Turn left on **King Road** as Lake Creek Road ends. Wind past old homesteads, some in mint condition, others in disrepair and covered with vegetation. At mile 7.7 the pavement ends. The road passes several farms and woodlots before narrowing, entering forest, and topping a summit at mile 11.4. Pavement resumes at mile 12.8. Occasional homes and clearings among the trees.

18.3 Bear left across creek on **W. Fir** in Winlock. Cross Highway 603.

18.4 Cross main-line railroad tracks and turn left on **First Street**. *Note: Cafe and grocery, half block to the right on First Street, are open all week.* Follow First Street uphill and around corner, and continue on **Rhoades Road** as it joins from the right. Mt. Rainier may appear to the northeast and Mt. St. Helens to the southeast as Rhoades Road wanders back and forth across upland pastures.

19.3 Continue on **Rhoades Road North** (dead end) as Rhoades Road turns right. Enter Winolequa Park at mile 19.7. Constructed by Winlock Jaycees and other citizens, this park was dedicated to the Vietnam veterans in 1975. A well-equipped kitchen shelter may be reserved for group use; contact Winlock City Hall for reservations. Return to Rhoades Road intersection.

20.0 Turn left (east) on **Rhoades Road** from Rhoades Road North.

21.2 Turn left on **Minkler Road** as Rhoades Road ends.

22.3 Bear right on **Sargent Road** as Minkler Road ends. St. Urban Church of the Assumption, built in 1891, on the right at mile 23.3. Cross I-5 on an overpass at mile 23.7.

24.3 Turn right on **Meier Road** as Park Road goes on.

25.3 Turn left on **Hart Road** and head down into a valley.

26.3 Continue on **Frost Road** as it joins from the right. Large grassy field surrounds a clump of oak, aspen, and ash trees.

27.9 Turn left on **Jackson Highway**. Wide, paved shoulder.

28.8 Turn left into Lewis and Clark State Park; camping, picnicking, kitchen shelters, and nature trail. Follow the loop drive around the park.

29.3 Leave park and turn left on **Jackson Highway**. Old-growth tree exhibit on left at mile 29.9; Jackson Courthouse Historic Site on right at 31.0. Cross U.S. 12 at mile 31.1.

31.4 Turn left on **Avery Road East** by Loggers World sign.

32.4 Turn right on **Keasling Road**.

33.4 Turn left on **Koontz Road** as Keasling ends. Roadside nurseries display fields of gladioli. Cross I-5 on an overpass at mile 35.0.

35.7 Turn left on **Jordan Road**. Cross main-line railroad tracks and Highway 603 at mile 37.1; continue on **Conrad Road** and coast downhill through forest. Vine maple adds a touch of brilliant color during a fall tour.

39.1 Turn right on **Pleasant Valley Road**. Enjoy six miles of delightful, relaxing riding.

45.4 Turn left on **Twin Oaks Road** as Pleasant Valley Road ends.

46.9 Turn right on **State Route 6** and cross the Chehalis River.

47.1 Turn left on **Bunker Creek Road** and enter Adna.

47.3 Turn right on **Dieckman Road**.

47.5 Turn right into Back Memorial Park; end of tour.

131 TOLEDO–TOUTLE

STARTING POINT: Toledo Community Park in Toledo. From the north take exit 63 from I-5, head east on State Route 505 for 2.6 miles to the Jackson Highway, and turn right (south) toward Toledo. Keep right on Fifth Street and turn right on Cedar Street, following signs to the park. Park entrance is on Sixth Street. From the south take exit 60 from I-5, head east on State Route 505 for 3.5 miles, then turn right on Fifth Street in Toledo. Keep right with Fifth Street and follow signs to the park as above. If park entrance is closed, park by ball diamond behind school, just north of park along Sixth Street.

DISTANCE: 46 miles.
TERRAIN: Hilly.
TOTAL CUMULATIVE ELEVATION GAIN: 1500 feet.
RECOMMENDED TIME OF YEAR: Any season.
RECOMMENDED STARTING TIME: 8 to 9 A.M.
ALLOW: 6 to 8 hours.
POINTS OF INTEREST
Lone Hill Cemetery
Toutle River flood damage
Mt. St. Helens Visitor Center

ELEVATION PROFILE

This tour may be taken at any season of the year, but a bright, clear, sunny day enhances the majestic appearances of Mt. Rainier and Mt. St. Helens, which command the horizon from many points along the way. Mt. Rainier dominates the northeastern Cascades as the tour follows the valley near the Cowlitz River. Mt. St. Helens joins the skyline as the route climbs to the plateau above the river. Lone Hill Cemetery provides an excellent vantage point for enjoying the splendor of the scene. Perched atop a narrow ridge above the Cowlitz River, this old cemetery dates back to the 1850s, when Washington Territory was first penetrated by settlers of European extraction. A monument at the cemetery entrance proclaims the friendship between the early pioneers and the Cowlitz Indians, who hunted the nearby prairie. Today the prairie is fenced and plowed and supports Christmas trees and cattle.

Oak and ash trees line the edges of Layton Prairie as the route joins State Route 505. Viewed from two successive road summits, the distant hillsides resemble a patchwork quilt pattern of browns and greens, the result of many years of clearcut logging operations. Summertime slash fires fill the air with the smell of smoke, as areas are readied for reforestation with tiny Douglas fir seedlings.

Tall firs line the road as the route heads west along the North Fork Toutle River. Suddenly the road bursts out of the forest, and the devastation of the Toutle River Valley appears. The eruption of Mt. St. Helens in May 1980 sent a wall of water and gray volcanic ash mud down this valley, sweeping everything in its path. The valley is still a wasteland of mounds of volcanic ash, but young alder trees have begun reforesting the edges.

Numerous ducks frequent the marshy edges of Silver Lake west of the little town of Toutle, while eagles soar over the foothills near Seaquest State Park. As the route climbs to the top of one of these hills, Mt. St. Helens emerges then disappears again, and the road plunges downhill toward I-5, where tall mounds of dredged-up volcanic ash furnish a reminder of the 1980 eruption

Mt. Rainier puts in one last appearance as the route briefly leaves the Cowlitz River lowland and runs along a side valley. As the route recrosses the Cowlitz River, it is not difficult to picture the old sternwheeler *Toledo* chuffing its way up from Longview to the upper landing and trading post that were the beginnings of the present town of Toledo.

MILEAGE LOG

0.0 Toledo Community Park. Leave park entrance and head east on **Cedar Street**.

0.2 Turn left on **First Street** as Cedar Street ends.

0.5 Turn right on **Augustus Street** as First Street ends, then right on **Cowlitz Street (State Route 505)**. Cross Cowlitz River on narrow, two-lane bridge. Continue uphill on S.R. 505 as Jackson Highway goes right at mile 1.0.

1.5 Turn left on **Collins Road**. Descend to the valley along the Cowlitz River. The road zigs and zags across the valley before climbing steeply uphill.

4.0 Bear left at unmarked wye, pedal uphill, and merge with **Eadon Road** (unmarked) at stop sign. Lone Hill Cemetery on the left at mile 5.8; magnificent views of Mt. St. Helens and Mt. Rainier.

6.5 Turn right on **Layton Road** as Eadon Road ends.

7.5 Turn left on **State Route 505** and pedal through prairie land. Cross Cedar Creek at 10.0 and climb to a summit at mile 10.8. Descend into a valley, cross Salmon Creek at 12.8, and top another summit at 15.0.

15.7 Turn right toward Toutle on **State Route 504**, and wind through a canyon of trees. Cross the South Fork Toutle River at mile 19.4.

20.0 Go through downtown Toutle; grocery store, post office, drive-in cafe, and restaurant. Cross marshy area at end of Silver Lake at mile 21.7 near Lakeside Cafe. Silver Lake Store at mile 22.4. Seaquest State Park at mile 25.0; picnicking and camping with hot showers, Mt. St. Helens National Volcanic Monument Visitor Center.

26.5 Turn right on **Schaffran Road** and pedal uphill to views of Mt. St. Helens.

29.1 Bear left on **Tower Road** as Schaffran Road ends.

29.2 Turn right on **State Route 504** and descend a long hill.

31.0 Turn right on **Old Pacific Highway** just before S.R. 504 crosses I-5; cafes and grocery. Cross Toutle River and I-5 at miles 33.6 and 33.9; road now marked **Barnes Drive**. Cowlitz River and main-line railroad tracks on the left.

37.1 Turn left on **Imboden Road** as Barnes Drive turns right and ascends a long hill. Road is renamed **Mandy Road** as it enters Lewis County

at mile 38.5.

39.2 Turn left with Mandy Road as Rogers Road continues on. I-5 crosses overhead at mile 41.5; fishing access along the Cowlitz River has chemical toilets.

42.0 Turn left on **Herriford Road** as Mandy heads up a short hill.

42.6 Turn left on **Jackson Highway**. Mt. Rainier looms over the country-side.

45.4 Turn left on **State Route 505** toward Toledo. Cross Cowlitz River and enter Toledo at mile 46.3.

45.9 Bear left on **Cowlitz Street** as S.R. 505 bends right and uphill.

46.0 Turn left on **Fifth Street** as Cowlitz ends.

46.1 Turn right on **Cedar Street**.

46.2 End of tour at Toledo Community Park.

"Naw — that happens only once every thousand years."

132 RAINBOW FALLS STATE PARK–SEAQUEST STATE PARK

STARTING POINT: Rainbow Falls State Park. Take I-5 to exit 77 (State Route 6), turn west, and proceed 16 miles to state park. After checking with park manager, leave cars in picnic area parking lot.

ALTERNATIVE STARTING POINT: (Shortens tour by 18 miles.) Back Memorial County Park in Adna, 4.5 miles west of I-5 on State Route 6. Turn right on Bunker Creek Road, then right on Dieckman Road to the park entrance.

DISTANCE: Day tours of 45, 52, 63, and 70 miles; first day of two-day tour, 34 to 51 miles; second day, 32 to 55 miles.
TERRAIN: Hilly.
TOTAL CUMULATIVE ELEVATION GAIN: 500 to 3500 feet: first day of two-day tour, 900 to 1900 feet; second day, 1200 to 1600 feet.
RECOMMENDED TIME OF YEAR: Any season, but road summits may be icy in winter.
RECOMMENDED STARTING TIME: 9 A.M.
ALLOW: 6 hours to 2 days.
POINTS OF INTEREST
Nostalgic Burma Shave signs
Historical Monument in Toledo
Mt. St. Helens Visitor Center

As the tour leaves Rainbow Falls State Park on the Chehalis River, it follows backroads and State Route 6 into the valley near Pe Ell. From there the route follows a tributary of the Chehalis River up to a pass and down to the South Fork Chehalis. Small farms contribute their part to the local economy, but it is the forested hillsides that produce the main crop of trees for the forest products industry. Logging roads take off right and left as the route climbs to a 600-foot summit before descending into the picturesque South Fork Chehalis River Valley. Another forested summit must be conquered before the route descends to Cougar Flats along Stillwater Creek. Freshly painted Burma Shave signs nudge the memories of those over 55, while nearby, blades spin on a brightly decorated windmill, its wind power generating little but pleasure for the beholder.

The little town of Vader supplies the needed calories to generate pedal power for continuing the tour south along the Cowlitz River. After another fuel stop in Castle Rock, several miles of backroad hill-climbing stand between the cyclist and the camping destination of Seaquest State Park, where the new Mt. St. Helens National Volcanic Monument Visitor Center

155

opened in 1993. Motels along the highway in Castle Rock offer alternative accommodations.

The return route to Rainbow Falls State Park runs along the eastern bank of the Cowlitz River to the next upstream bridge at Toledo. Close inspection of the river shows several miles of fishing access provided by the Washington State Department of Wildlife. A broad, freely flowing river as it joins the Columbia at Kelso-Longview, the Cowlitz River provided the main means of transportation into the prairies and forests of Washington Territory. Sternwheelers plied the river upstream to the historic Cowlitz Landing near the present town of Toledo, which was named after one of the riverboats. A monument near the bridge commemorates the convention held in 1851 that drafted a petition to the U.S. Congress to divide the Oregon Territory and establish a separate territory north of the Columbia River.

Leaving Toledo, the route continues over prairie that was claimed through the Donation Land Claim Act of 1850. Magnificent views of Mt. Rainier and Mt. St. Helens greeted the settlers of yesterday as they do bicycle tourists of today.

As are other towns along this tour, Winlock is situated deep in a valley, along the banks of King and Olequa creeks. A steep hill separates it from the Napavine Prairie. The route climbs this hill and traverses a bit of the prairie before following the pleasant valley of Stearns Creek to join the Chehalis Valley at Claquato. Acres of oats, wheat, corn, and peas flourish in the fertile soil near Adna, terminus of one of the shorter versions of this tour.

The impact of busy traffic along State Route 6 is softened by smoothly paved shoulders on the last hill of this tour, and a viewpoint lined with old masonry guardrails offers a break shortly before a backroad route leaves the highway toward the back gate of Rainbow Falls State Park.

MILEAGE LOG

FIRST DAY

0.0 Rainbow Falls State Park. Proceed north through the park, around the back gate, and turn left on **Leudinghaus Road**. *Note: For alternate starting directions from Adna, see end of mileage log.*

1.0 Turn left on **Chandler Road** at T junction.

1.3 Cross the Chehalis River and turn right on **Doty-Dryad Road** just before Chandler intersects highway. Acute-angled railroad crossing at mile 2.1.

2.7 Turn left on **Stevens Road** at stop sign in Doty as Doty-Dryad is marked Dead End.

3.1 Cross railroad tracks and turn right on **State Route 6**. Road shoulder is smooth and generous as it turns and climbs over the hill into the Pe Ell Valley.

6.4 Bear left on **Mauerman Road** as S.R. 6 continues to Pe Ell.

7.4 Turn left on **Pe Ell-McDonald Road** as Mauerman Road ends. The road follows a creek valley and heads uphill to a summit at mile 10.4, continuing through forest and rolling countryside.

16.3 Turn right on **Wildwood Road** by corner grocery as Pe Ell-McDonald

Road ends. Pedal through the South Fork Chehalis River Valley, past farms and historic cemeteries, before climbing a ten percent grade to a summit at mile 26.1.

28.3   Turn left on **State Route 506** toward I-5 and Vader as a directional sign points right 1.5 miles to Ryderwood. Watch for Burma Shave signs, gaily painted windmill, and horse-drawn farm implements on display. *Note: Winlock-Vader Road goes left to Winlock at 32.3, cuts 42 miles off full tour.* Pass through Vader at mile 32.7; grocery and cafe. Cross main-line railroad tracks.

33.5   Turn right at top of steep hill as S. Military Road goes left. Tremendous views of Mt. Rainier and Mt. St. Helens. On a clear day a small section of Mt. Adams shows up behind the distant foothills. *Note: To shorten this tour by 40 miles, do not turn right, but continue on S.R. 506 1.1 miles, turning left on Telegraph Road to join Knowles Road at mile 23.7 of second-day tour log.* Enter Cowlitz County at mile 34.7. Climb a short hill and cross bridge over main-line railroad tracks at mile 35.8. Route follows Cowlitz River for several miles.

43.0   Turn left toward Castle Rock at blinking red light by grocery as PH 10 Road goes right and State Route 411 continues on. Pass Castle Rock Fairgrounds, cross Cowlitz River, and enter Castle Rock on **A Street**.

43.7   Turn left on **Front Stree**t past cafe and grocery in downtown Castle Rock. Continue on **Huntington Avenue** as it joins from the right, and climb out of town along the river. Cross I-5 at mile 44.5 and continue uphill past motels on wide shoulder of **State Route 504 (Spirit Lake Highway)**.

46.5   Turn left on **Tower Road** by gas-grocery. Immediately bear right on **Schaffran Road** and continue uphill. Views of Mt. St. Helens at summit.

49.2   Turn left on **State Route 504**.

50.4   Turn right to Mt. St. Helens National Volcanic Monument Visitor Center (mile 50.6). Extensive displays of history, geology, and volcanic eruption. Continue past visitor center on frontage road.

50.8   Turn left into Seaquest State Park; camping, picnicking, shelters, group camp.

SECOND DAY

0.0   Leave Seaquest State Park entrance and turn right on **State Route 504**.

5.5   Turn right on **Pacific Highway North** just before S.R. 504 crosses I-5. Cross Toutle River and I-5 at miles 8.0 and 8.3. Road now named **Barnes Drive**. Cowlitz River and main-line railroad tracks appear on the left.

11.5   Turn left on **Imboden Road** as Barnes Drive ascends a long hill. Road enters Lewis County at mile 13.6.

13.8   Turn left with **Mandy Road**. I-5 crosses overhead at mile 16.1. Fishing access along Cowlitz River has chemical toilets.

16.6   Turn left on **Herriford Road** as Mandy heads up a short hill.

17.2   Turn left on **Jackson Highway**. Mt. Rainier on the eastern horizon.

20.0   Turn left on **State Route 505** toward Toledo. Cross Cowlitz River and enter Toledo at mile 20.3; grocery and cafe.

20.5   Keep right with S.R. 505 as Cowlitz Street goes left. Toledo Community Park is 0.3 mile from this intersection at Cedar and Sixth streets. See detail map, Tour 131, page 153.

20.6   Continue on **Fifth Street** as it joins from the left. Signs point back on Fifth Street toward Community Park, 0.5 mile.

20.8   Turn left on **Ash Street** by grocery–fishing tackle store toward Vader and Ryderwood. The road is shortly renamed **Toledo-Vader Road**. Climb up to open prairie.

21.5   Turn right on **Drews Prairie Road**.

22.9   Turn left with Drews Prairie Road as Camus Road goes right. Descend a short hill, go under I-5 at mile 23.5, and climb up to the prairie again.

23.7   Turn right at top of hill on **Knowles Road** toward Winlock. I-5 traffic dashes past on the right. Road pulls away from I-5 and starts uphill through forest at mile 25.0.

26.2   Turn left at stop sign on **Highway 603**.

26.5   Turn right on **No. Military Road** toward Winlock High School.

27.3   Turn left on **Nevil Road** just past the high school. Acres of sheared Christmas trees.

29.5   Bear right on **Highway 603** at Winlock city limits. Pass a grocery and cross N.E. First Street; cafe one block right on First.

29.7   Cross main-line railroad tracks. At stop sign, cross Kerron Avenue and continue on **W. Walnut Street.**

29.8   Cross Olequa Creek and immediately turn right on **N.W. Arden Avenue.**

29.9   Continue on **N.E. King Road** at crossing of Fir Street.

30.1   Turn right on **N.W. Dexter Avenue** past Lewis County Public Works as N.E. King Road continues uphill.

30.2   Turn left with thoroughfare as it is renamed **N.W. Byham Road.**

30.4   Turn right on **Tennessee Road**, cross King Creek, and head uphill.

33.7   Turn left on **Pleasant Valley Road** as Tennessee ends.

41.3   Turn left on **Twin Oaks Road** toward Pe Ell as Pleasant Valley Road ends.

42.7   Turn left on **State Route 6**. *Note: For Adna return, turn right on S.R. 6, cross bridge, turn left into Adna on Bunker Creek Road, then right on Dieckman Road to Back Memorial Park.* Traffic will pick up along this road. Cross South Fork Chehalis River at 46.5 and acute-angled railroad tracks at mile 46.8.

49.8   Turn right on **River Road**. Old stone guardrails along the road next to river.

52.0   Turn right across the Chehalis River on **Meskill Road**, then immediately left on **Leudinghaus Road**.

54.7   Turn left into Rainbow Falls State Park back entrance and go past entrance gate through pedestrian opening.

54.8   End of tour by picnic area.

ALTERNATIVE STARTING POINT MILEAGE LOG

0.0   Head out of Back Memorial Park on entrance road and turn left on **Dieckman Road**.

0.3   Turn left on **Bunker Creek Road**.

0.4   Turn right on **State Route 6** and cross the Chehalis River. Watch for acute-angled railroad tracks at mile 1.0.

4.7   Cross the South Fork Chehalis River and turn left on **Boistfort Road**.

10.8   Continue on **Wildwood Road** as Pe Ell-McDonald Road goes right. Continue on main mileage log at mile 16.3.

133 LONG BEACH PENINSULA

STARTING POINT: Fort Canby State Park. From the north, take exit 104 (U.S. 101) from I-5 in Olympia and continue on State Route 8 and U.S. 12 to Montesano. Follow State Route 107 to rejoin U.S. 101 and continue south to Ilwaco. Prominent signs direct the traveler on Loop 100 and Spur 100 to Fort Canby State Park. From the south take exit 39 (State Route 4) from I-5 in Kelso. Follow State Route 4 to where it joins U.S. 101. Continue south to Ilwaco and Fort Canby State Park.

DISTANCE: 43 miles.
TERRAIN: Flat with one hill.
TOTAL CUMULATIVE ELEVATION GAIN: 520 feet.
RECOMMENDED TIME OF YEAR: Any season.
RECOMMENDED STARTING TIME: 9 A.M.
ALLOW: 6 hours.
POINTS OF INTEREST
Lewis and Clark Interpretive Center
Fort Canby State Park
Old homes and church in Oysterville
Cranberry bogs

ELEVATION PROFILE

From its junction with the mainland at the mouth of the Columbia River, the Long Beach Peninsula extends its narrow finger north for 25 miles, protecting the calm waters of Willapa Bay from the frequently storm-tossed waters of the Pacific Ocean. Cape Disappointment, the peninsula's southern extension, forms the high bluff of forested land where the Columbia River flows into the Pacific Ocean. It was first charted in 1775 by Spanish explorers but received its name from the British fur trader John Meares, who tried but failed to find a navigable channel into the mouth of the great river in 1788. American explorer Captain Robert Gray succeeded in crossing the bar in 1792 and entered the river, naming it after his ship. In the fall of 1805 the Lewis and Clark expedition, having traveled westward from the Mississippi River, viewed the Pacific Ocean from atop Cape Disappointment. The history of this most successful of American explorations is presented in detail at the interpretive center in Fort Canby State Park. Cape Disappointment was selected as the site of a lighthouse in 1850, and the light went into operation in 1856. A second lighthouse went up on North Head in 1898, and both are still important aids to navigation. The area was proclaimed a military reservation in 1852 and officially named Fort Canby in honor of General Edward Richard Sprigg Canby in 1875.

Over the years, barracks and fortifications with mortars and rifles have been installed and removed; a minefield was even activated during World War II. Remains of the concrete bunkers are still in evidence. In 1947 Fort Canby was declared surplus property and placed in the custody of the U.S. Army Corps of Engineers. During the next year, 491 acres were transferred to the U.S. Coast Guard, while the Washington State Parks and Recreation Commission leased and purchased land for a state park.

SCALE OF MILES
0   1   2   3

Crossing the Columbia Bar has always been a difficult maneuver for ships, and many have run aground or capsized in the stormy waters. The Coast Guard maintains a lifeboat station east of the North Jetty with a motor-lifeboat surf school for training coastguard personnel. Visitors to the state park may have a chance to observe these young people learning their trade as their boats are tossed by the waves breaking over the bar.

Several towns dot the Long Beach Peninsula. Ilwaco, at the south end, supports the commercial and charter fishing industries, while Seaview and Long Beach are oriented toward beach tourism and summer and retirement homes. Nahcotta, on the Willapa Bay side of the peninsula, is an important center for the propagation and harvesting of oysters. Nearby cranberry bogs cover many acres and represent an important part of the cranberry industry in Washington State. Oysterville, founded in 1854 near the northern end of the peninsula, has been placed on the National Register of Historic Places. Several houses and a church built in the 1890s remain as fine examples of the architecture of that era. The excellent restoration and maintenance of these buildings bear testimony to the pride and industry of today's Oysterville townspeople.

Leadbetter Point State Park on the northern tip of the peninsula and nearby Willapa National Wildlife Refuge offer important natural habitats for waterfowl such as the black brant goose, Caspian tern, and snowy plover.

MILEAGE LOG

0.0   Fort Canby State Park parking area by rest rooms. Proceed out of park past park office and turn left at stop sign on **Spur 100**, up the hill toward Ilwaco.

0.7   Bear left on **Loop 100** as Spur 100 ends.

1.4   Turn left toward North Head Lighthouse on **North Head Lighthouse Road**.

1.9   Turn left down gravel path to North Head Lighthouse. Sweeping views of beach and surf toward the mouth of the Columbia River. Return to the road.

2.4   Turn left again to a viewpoint. Trails lead around the fort's old lookout bunkers. Return to main road.

3.4   Turn left on main road and head downhill.

4.8   Turn left on **Willows Road** and continue downhill. The road bends right at mile 5.7 and is renamed **30 Street**.

5.8   Turn left on **L Place** in Seaview. As it enters Long Beach at mile 7.0 the road is renamed **California**.

7.4   Turn left on **10th SW** as California ends, then right on **Boulevard South**.

7.8   Jog right on **Bolstad**, then left on **Boulevard North**. Main access to the proclaimed World's Longest Beach is to the left through an archway. Long Beach shopping area to the right; bakery, cafes.

9.2   Turn right on **26th NW (95 Street)**, then left on **State Route 103**. Entrance to Loomis Lake State park is on the left at mile 13.6.

17.4   Continue on **Vernon Avenue** as S.R. 103 turns right in Ocean Park. Entrance to Pacific Pines State Park is on the left at mile 18.1.

18.9 Turn left on **Joe Johns Road**, then right at stop sign on **N Place**, which bends left and is marked **295 Street**. Road bends right at 19.5 and becomes **G Street**. Pedal through Surfside Estates. Road bends right at mile 21.7 and becomes **338 Place**.

21.8 Turn left on **I Street** at stop sign.

21.9 Turn right on **Oysterville Road** and pedal over sand ridge. *Note: At mile 22.7 Stackpole Road goes left 4.8 miles to Leadbetter Point State Park.* Oysterville Store and Post Office (oldest post office in Washington State) on the right at mile 23.0.

23.2 Cross Territory Road in Oysterville and follow around loop past oyster company buildings.

23.6 Cross Oysterville Road and continue on **Territory Road**. Signs date old homes, schoolhouse, and church in Oysterville.

24.1 Bear left on **Sandridge Road (State route 103)**. Restaurant, county park, and grocery on the left in Nahcotta at mile 27.1. Oyster farming facilities nearby.

27.7 Continue on Sandridge Road as S.R. 103 turns right to Ocean Park. Cranberry warehouse and bogs on right at mile 34.8. Cross U.S. 101 at mile 39.3.

40.3 Join **U.S. 101** as it merges from right, and pedal past Ilwaco municipal water supply (Black Lake). Memorial to World War II casualties.

41.0 Turn right on **Spruce Street** in Ilwaco, then immediately left on **Loop 100 (Second Street)**.

42.7 Turn left on **Spur 100** at stop sign.

43.2 Turn right by Fort Canby park office.

43.4 End of tour at picnic area parking lot.

"You know, I have never seen a bird in this area."

134 LEWIS RIVER

STARTING POINT: Public parking area at the corner of Davidson Avenue and Second Street in Woodland. Take exit 21 from I-5 (Woodland, Lake Merwin) into Woodland and follow Goerig Street and Davidson Avenue to parking lot.

ALTERNATIVE STARTING POINT: Port of Kalama Marina parking lot; extends ride by 29 miles. See Tour 135.

DISTANCE: Total, 56 miles: first day, 20 miles; second day, 36 miles. Alternative starting point, 85 miles: first day, 39 miles; second day, 46 miles.
TERRAIN: Hilly.
TOTAL CUMULATIVE ELEVATION GAIN: 3150 feet: first day, 1350 feet; second day, 1800 feet.

RECOMMENDED TIME OF YEAR: March through October.
RECOMMENDED STARTING TIME: 9 to 10 A.M.
ALLOW: 6 to 7 hours; 1 to 2 days.
POINTS OF INTEREST
Views along Lewis River
Battle Ground Lake State Park

ELEVATION PROFILE

When traced back from its junction with the Columbia River near Woodland, the Lewis River retreats quickly into a series of wild canyons and hydroelectric reservoirs. Steep canyon walls discourage extensive development of recreational property, and timber interests control much of the adjoining countryside, keeping traffic light on county roads. With the bonus of the relatively unspoiled scenery, this is a great back-country tour.

Several parks line the course of this tour. Horseshoe Lake Park in Woodland takes the name of a lake formed when a bend in the Lewis River was bypassed. Although the river now flows straight past the town, the county boundary still follows the original river course through this oxbow lake. Where the tour route crosses the east fork of the river, Clark County's Daybreak Park offers a place to relax along the rippling water. At a bend in the road along the East Fork Lewis River, Clark County has acquired extensive river frontage by Moulton Falls. These parks, although of interest, are secondary to the main objective of this tour—Battle Ground Lake State

Park. The lake occupies the basin of a crater with no surface tributary or outlet: underground springs and sinks keep the water clear and fresh for swimming. Park trails and entrance road climb the rim of the crater and descend to the water's edge. Drive-in and walk-in campsites, coin-operated hot showers, and kitchen shelters in the central park area support a wide range of activities. A group camp, available by reservation with the park manager, offers Adirondack shelters, tables, fire pits, and the environmental benefits of an adjoining railroad. For cyclists not interested in camping, a nearby bed-and-breakfast establishment offers more luxurious accommodations. (See index of tours with bed-and-breakfast accommodations.)

Although hills abound on this ride, the scenery makes them all worthwhile. The wild rapids and falls of the pea-green Lewis River and its tributaries, rippling and splashing their way through dense forests, are a favorite habitat of the water ouzel. Wintering tundra swans, their cries sounding like children at play, fly up from a quiet bend of the river. Acres of daffodils identify bulb farms along the main fork of the Lewis River, and herds of deer graze the pastures and roadsides. The countryside is slow to change, making this a delightful tour.

MILEAGE LOG

FIRST DAY

0.0 City of Woodland public parking lot. Turn left on **Davidson Avenue** and follow the thoroughfare as it is renamed **Goerig Street**. Continue under I-5 at mile 0.4.

0.6 Turn right toward La Center and Amboy and cross Lewis River.

0.9 Bear right at wye on **N.W. Pacific Highway** toward La Center.

6.1 Turn left on **E. 4th Street** toward Amboy in La Center city center; grocery. As it leaves La Center, road is renamed **N.E. Lockwood Creek Road.**

8.2 Turn right on **N.E. 40th Avenue** at the top of a steep hill. View of Mt. St. Helens. Road name changes to **N.E. Charity Road** at mile 8.9.

9.6 Bear right on **J.A. Moore Road**. As the road executes several bends it is renamed **N.E. 61st Avenue, N.E. Bennett Road,** and **N.E. 269th Street.**

12.5 Bear right on **N.E. Daybreak Road** toward Battle Ground and cross the East Fork Lewis River. Go through Daybreak Park at mile 12.6 as road is renamed **N.E. 82nd Avenue.**

13.0 Turn left at T junction on **N.E. 259th Street**. As the road bends, it is renamed **N.E. Manley Road**. At top of hill, road is renamed **N.E. 92nd Avenue.**

14.3 Turn left on **N.E. 239th Street** at T junction. View of Mt. St. Helens.

15.3 Turn left on **N.E. 112th Avenue** as N.E. 239th Street ends. Road bends right and becomes **N.E. 244th Street**. Cross N.E. Lewisville Highway (State Route 503) at mile 16.1.

16.5 Turn left on **N.E. 132nd Avenue** as N.E. 244th Street ends.

16.8 Turn right on **N.E. 249th Street** by Sacred Heart Cemetery as N.E. Dublin Road (dead end) continues. Road executes right and left

SCALE OF MILES

SCALE OF MILES

bends and is renamed **N.E. 152nd Avenue**, **N.E. 244th Street**, **N.E. Palmer Road**, and **N.E. 182nd Avenue**.

19.6   Turn left on **N.E. 249th Street** into Battle Ground Lake State Park. *Note: To visit group camp, do not turn on N.E. 249th Street, but continue on N.E. 182nd Avenue for 0.5 mile, turn left on N.E. 259th Street, cross railroad tracks, and turn left into group camp entrance road.* Nearest grocery is 1.8 miles into next day's ride; next nearest is in Battle Ground.

SECOND DAY

0.0   Leave Battle Ground Lake State Park entrance on **N.E. 249th Street** and turn left (north) on **N.E. 182nd Avenue**.

1.5   Bear left with thoroughfare on **N.E. 279th Street** as 182nd Avenue ends. Grocery at mile 1.8.

2.0   Turn right with thoroughfare on **N.E. 172nd Avenue**. Cross East Fork of Lewis River at mile 2.6.

2.7   Turn right on **N.E. Lucia Falls Road**. *Note: Bed-and-breakfast location 2.5 miles farther along route.* Clark County Moulton Falls Park at mile 8.2, rest rooms at mile 8.4. Road name changes to **N.E. Railroad Avenue** as N.E. Sunset Falls Road goes right at mile 8.5.

11.1   Turn left on **E. Yacolt Road** in Yacolt as Railroad Avenue ends, then immediately turn right toward Amboy on **S. Amboy Road**. Cafe and grocery.

15.6   Turn left on **N.E. 399th Street** (**State Route 503**) by tavern and restaurant in Amboy. Cross creek and climb short hill.

15.9   Go straight with N.E. 399th Street by cafe and grocery as S.R. 503 swings left. Museum and community park at mile 16.0. Climb a long, steep hill.

19.3   Turn right on **N.E. Munch Road** as N.E. Graham Road continues. A long downhill ensues.

21.6   Turn right toward Amboy on **N.E. Cedar Creek Road** at base of hill. Cross Cedar Creek and turn left on **Pup Creek Road** toward Green Mountain School and Green Mountain Baptist Church.

24.1   Continue on **N.E. Grinnell Road** as it enters from right. Road name changes to **N.E. Etna Road** at mile 24.4. Pass Cedar Creek Boat Launching Ramp at mile 28.2.

29.4   Bear right on **N.E. Cedar Creek Road** as Etna Road ends. Road name changes to **N.E. Hayes Road** at mile 30.5.

35.4   Bear right at wye toward Woodland and cross Lewis River as N.W. Pacific Highway goes left.

35.7   Turn left on **State Route 503** into Woodland. As it enters town the road becomes **Goerig Street**. Follow thoroughfare as it bends right and is renamed **Davidson Avenue**.

36.3   Turn right into public parking lot; end of tour.

COWLITZ COUNTY

135 KALAMA–WOODLAND

STARTING POINT: Port of Kalama Marina parking lot in Kalama. Take exit 30 from I-5 into Kalama, 2.5 hours driving time from Seattle. Turn right at west end of overpass and follow signs to marina along Hendrickson Drive.

DISTANCE: 35 miles.
TERRAIN: Flat to moderate.
TOTAL CUMULATIVE ELEVATION GAIN: 300 feet.
RECOMMENDED TIME OF YEAR: Any season; spring best for flowers.
RECOMMENDED STARTING TIME: Not critical.
ALLOW: 2 to 6 hours.
POINTS OF INTEREST
Lilac garden and bulb farm in Woodland
Views along Columbia and Lewis rivers

ELEVATION PROFILE

In April 1976, the Washington State Highway Commission instituted a six-month trial of a bikeway along the shoulder of Interstate 5 between the Dike Road Interchange north of Woodland and the Todd Road Interchange south of Kalama. The experiment proved successful (no reported casualties), and this bikeway is now available to bicyclists as are most of the rural interstate shoulders in Washington. Bikeway rules include use of the right-hand shoulder in daylight hours only and conformity with bike route regulations. Experiences using this bikeway have been surprisingly nontraumatic. Compared with shoulderless secondary highways, it is almost idyllic, the traffic noise being the only major liability.

Noises of the freeway are left far behind when the route descends to Dike Access Road and heads across the delta to the Columbia River. Levees and pumping stations along the river keep the fertile land from flooding. Oat and wheat stubble provides winter forage for large flocks of Canada geese as well as smaller flocks of tundra and trumpeter swans. Large herds of dairy cattle graze the lush green pastures and stare at unfamiliar two-wheeled intruders. Meadowlarks flush from alongside the roads, singing as they fly away. Red-winged blackbirds seek out nesting sites in the cattails. A red-tailed hawk carefully surveys the territory from his perch atop an old piling.

Big ocean-going ships, decks piled high with container freight, move slowly through the broad waters of the Columbia on their way up the river to Portland as tugs push sawdust-piled barges down the river. A pulp mill across the river in St. Helens, Oregon, sends plumes of fog into the atmosphere.

Groves of cottonwood and alder trees line many of the delta roads, while swamp dogwoods, snowberries, blackberry vines, and horsetails fill in the wet spots. Tulips, daffodils and Dutch irises put on a colorful spring spectacle at the Holland America Bulb Farms' many acres of rich delta soil near Woodland. Woodland is also known for the Hulda Klager Lilac Gardens, which date back to the turn of the century. Along with the hybridized lilacs are many flowers and exotic trees. The gardens are open all year, but are especially beautiful when the lilacs bloom in spring. Garry oak thrives around Horseshoe Lake in Woodland, where a city park provides picnicking and swimming. Restaurants and grocery stores are nearby.

The rapid return trip to Kalama via the five miles of freeway brings no surprises except a corpse or two of small animals such as opossum, raccoon, and barn owl. Energetic cyclists who elect to climb over Green Mountain are rewarded with a spectacular view of the Woodland-Kalama delta, including the giant heat exchanger of the decommissioned Trojan Nuclear Power Plant with its strobe-light warning beacon rising high above the Columbia River near Rainier, Oregon.

MILEAGE LOG

0.0 Parking lot by Port of Kalama Marina office in Kalama. Leave parking area and follow **Marine Drive** around lagoon.

0.2 Turn right on **Hendrickson Drive**, then immediately right again into waterfront park. Go past rest rooms and totem pole and turn left on paved trail along the Columbia River.

0.7 Turn right on **Hendrickson Drive** as trail ends. Beware of several acute-angled railroad spurs crossing roadway. Cross main-line railroad tracks at mile 2.1 as road bends left and right and is renamed **Toteff Road**.

2.3 Turn right up **I-5** access ramp and continue along shoulder.

7.0 Bear right on exit 22 ramp and leave freeway. Turn right on **Dike Access Road** at foot of ramp.

"No, thanks, I think I'd rather walk it."

8.9 Bear left at wye on **Dike Road**. Road bends left alongside railroad tracks at mile 14.2 and becomes **Kuhnis Road**.

17.0 Turn right on **Whalen Loop Road** and cross railroad tracks as Kuhnis ends.

17.5 Turn right on **South Pekin Road** by apex of Horseshoe Lake. *Note: Hulda Klager Lilac Gardens are 0.5 mile to the left on S. Pekin Road.* Pass Holland America Bulb Farms at mile 18.6.

19.8 End of paved road by Washington State Department of Wildlife fishing access on Lewis River. *Note: Signed conservation park; conservation license required for use of facilities.* Pekin Road continues on other side of river, inaccessible by bicycle. Turn around and go back along Pekin Road.

21.8 Turn right on **Pinkerton Drive** and pedal past ends of Horseshoe Lake. Road name changes to **Lake Shore Drive** by second arm of lake. Horseshoe Park (city of Woodland) on left at 22.7. A memorial plaque is dedicated to a friendly Indian named Zack.

23.1 Turn right on **Goerig Street** and follow main thoroughfare out of town. As it goes under I-5, road is designated **State Route 503**. Continue on S.R. 503 past Oak Tree Restaurant.

23.9 Continue past end of high retaining wall along Lewis River and turn left on **N. Goerig Street**. Ignore an earlier Goerig turnoff by drive-in. *Note: For the adventuresome and hardy, Green Mountain Road goes right at mile 24.7 up long, very steep hills, eventually leading back to Kalama; additional elevation gain 1000 to 2000 feet. For this you are on your own.*

25.1 Turn right onto approach to **I-5** and proceed along shoulder.

29.8 Leave freeway at exit 27, turn right on **Robb Road**, then immediately left on **Old Pacific Highway**. Enter Kalama on **S.E. 1st Street**.

32.4 Turn left under I-5 on **Elm Street** at south edge of Kalama business district, then right on **W. Frontage Road** toward Port Office and RV Park.

33.3 Turn left at stop sign on **Oak Street**. Cross bridge over railroad tracks and turn right toward Port of Kalama. Follow roadway as it circles around under bridge and is named **Hendrickson Drive**.

34.4 Bear right on **Marine Drive** into Port of Kalama Marina. End of tour at mile 34.6.

136   CASTLE ROCK–TOUTLE (Toutle River)

STARTING POINT: Park-and-ride lot near I-5 east of Castle Rock. Take exit 49 from I-5 and park in lot at southwest corner of interchange.

DISTANCE: 37 miles.
TERRAIN: Strenuous hills.
TOTAL CUMULATIVE ELEVATION GAIN: 1900 feet.
RECOMMENDED TIME OF YEAR: March through November.
RECOMMENDED STARTING TIME: 9 to 10 A.M.
ALLOW: 5 to 6 hours.
POINTS OF INTEREST
Tower Cemetery
Toutle River devastation
Mt. St. Helens Visitor Center

ELEVATION PROFILE

This relatively short but strenuous tour takes the bicyclist into a sparsely settled territory of Cowlitz County along the Toutle River northeast of Castle Rock. A traverse of an equally uninhabited hillside area southeast of town precedes the journey along Silver Lake and on to the Toutle.

Castle Rock is almost surrounded by the Cowlitz River as it swings around and heads south toward the Columbia, eight miles away. Farmland, Burlington Northern main-line tracks, and six lanes of I-5 share the narrow corridor of land between the Cowlitz River and the steep, forested hillsides to the east. Our tour views this part of the Cowlitz Valley before climbing into the hills on Headquarters Road. Large second-growth alder and bigleaf maple are the principal trees, though a few Douglas fir grow among the deciduous varieties. The route continues uphill to an intersection with Silver Lake Road, where the plunge to the Silver Lake plateau begins. Several small stump ranches enjoy a magnificent view of Mt. St. Helens and Mt. Rainier from their location high above Silver Lake. The Mt. St. Helens Volcanic National Monument Visitor Center offers displays of geology, history, and natural history of the region, as well as slide shows of the Mt. St. Helens eruption. Seaquest State Park occupies a half mile of Silver Lake's marshy shoreline, where bird watchers may have an opportunity for close encounters with nesting ducks as State Route 504 crosses a corner of the lake on a narrow causeway.

The North Fork Toutle River snuggles up to the highway as the route continues east through tall evergreen forest. Soon the route heads uphill again on Tower Road, where young tree plantings in logged-off areas speak of good forest management. As the road proceeds up and down the hills beside the Toutle River, aspen and oak trees, all hung with lichen, intersperse the fir and alder. Breaks in the trees reveal a cliff overlooking the muddy Toutle, while on the other side of the road, cattle ranches straddle the upland pastures. A section of the original road, undermined by the 1980

Mt. St. Helens mudflow, has been bypassed by a new road farther from the river. Eventually the road dives down to a crossing of the Toutle on a new concrete bridge. Cowlitz County maintains a cemetery on one of the many rolling hills that remain to be negotiated before the route again reaches State Route 504 and the final two-mile-long plunge to Castle Rock.

MILEAGE LOG

0.0 Leave park-and-ride lot and turn left (west) on **Huntington Avenue** into Castle Rock.

0.4 Bear right on **Front Avenue W.** through city center.

1.2 Turn right on **Huntington Avenue** as Front Avenue ends. Pass monument to early settlers by the city's namesake rocky monolith; trails up to viewpoint on the rock along the Cowlitz River. Lions Pride Park along the Cowlitz River at mile 1.5.

2.2 Turn right on **Pleasant Hill Road** as Huntington Avenue approaches I-5.

4.1 Turn left on **Headquarters Road** and start up a long, moderately steep hill. Top a summit at mile 7.2.

8.2 Turn left on **Davis Spur Road**.

8.4 Turn left on **S. Silver Lake Road** as Davis Spur ends.

12.3 Turn right on **State Route 504** by tavern/cafe. Mt. St. Helens appears occasionally on the horizon, topping the green hillsides.

14.0 Turn right on frontage road toward Mt. St. Helens Volcanic National Monument Visitor Center.

14.1 Stop at visitor center to view displays. Continue on frontage road.

14.4 Turn right on **State Route 504**. Seaquest State Park entrance across highway. Continue through Toutle at mile 18.9; grocery, cafes. Cross Toutle River at 19.9.

22.5 Turn left on **Tower Road** and start up through rolling hills and well-managed tree farms. Cross Toutle River on high bridge at 31.3. Tower Cemetery on right at 32.6. Rolling hills, steep in places.

35.6 Turn right on **State Route 504** by corner grocery, and speed down long hill. Cross I-5 on overpass and turn left into park-and-ride; end of tour.

137 CASTLE ROCK–LONGVIEW

STARTING POINT: Lions Pride Park along the Cowlitz River south of Castle Rock. Take exit 49 (State Route 504, Castle Rock) from I-5 and follow Huntington Avenue through Castle Rock to the park.

ALTERNATIVE STARTING POINT: Intersection of Hemlock Street and Kessler Boulevard by rest rooms of Sacajawea Park in Longview. Take exit 36 (State Route 432) from I-5 toward Longview. Turn right on Oregon Avenue at traffic light where S.R. 432 ends, and immediately turn left on Kessler Boulevard. Follow Kessler to Hemlock Street by rest rooms. Park along Kessler by Sacajawea Park.

DISTANCE: 33 miles.
TERRAIN: Combination of hilly, moderate, and flat.
TOTAL CUMULATIVE ELEVATION GAIN: 1300 feet.
RECOMMENDED TIME OF YEAR: Any season.
RECOMMENDED STARTING TIME: 10 A.M.
ALLOW: 4 hours.
POINTS OF INTEREST
Sacajawea Park in Longview
Views of Cowlitz River

ELEVATION PROFILE

Leaving Castle Rock, the route crosses the Cowlitz River and winds up the Delameter Creek Valley past homes, farms, and forest. Delameter Creek meanders by, crossing under the roadway several times. Wildflowers and gardens produce a blaze of color. Swallows swoop and dart along the road, snapping up insects on the wing. Roadway cuts reveal a bright reddish brown soil. The hard work put into the long climb is finally rewarded as the road suddenly curves over a summit and plunges down into the Coal Creek Valley. To avoid another highway at the terminus of Coal Creek Road, the route swerves onto Pacific Way and traverses the hillside along a system of sloughs leading into Longview and Sacajawea Park. Lake Sacajawea, the major feature of the park, is an oxbow lake formed from past meanderings of the Cowlitz and dredged out and kept from flooding by interconnection with Longview's system of canals, pumps, dikes, and levees. The park is attractively landscaped, with graveled jogging and cycling trails on the perimeter.

The return route to Castle Rock threads its way through Longview and Kelso on low-traffic side streets, plays leapfrog with I-5, and follows Pleasant Hill Road, a name appropriate for a road with pleasant scenery, very little traffic, and almost no hills. Side roads lead left and right, some with signs inviting passersby to fish for smelt, purchase nursery plants, or browse among the headstones of an old cemetery. Eventually Pleasant Hill Road ends, and Huntington Avenue, an almost-deserted stretch of Old Highway 99, leads back to the starting point along the Cowlitz River.

SCALE OF MILES

N

MILEAGE LOG

0.0 Starting from Lions Pride Park, turn left into Castle Rock on **Huntington Avenue.**

0.3 Turn left on **Front Avenue S.W.** by historical marker commemorating pioneers of the Castle Rock area. *Note: Trails lead from here to a ledge on the high rock (Castle Rock) overlooking the Cowlitz River.*

0.8 Turn left on **A Street** and cross the Cowlitz River.

1.5 Turn left on **State Route 411 (West Side Highway).**

2.2 Bear right and uphill on **Delameter Road.** Proceed up Delameter Valley past farms and homes. Road crosses creek several times.

8.2 Bear left with thoroughfare on **Woodside Drive** as Delameter Spur continues on to dead end. Grade becomes steeper, culminating in a summit at mile 9.6, then plunges down other side. Views of Mt. St. Helens, Mt. Rainier, and Mt. Adams near the summit.

11.2 Continue on **Coal Creek Road** as it merges from the right. Coal Creek General Store on right at mile 12.6.

14.5 Turn left on **Pacific Way** at bottom of hill and enter Longview.

19.5 Cross railroad tracks, turn left on **State Route 4 (Ocean Beach Highway),** then turn right on **Nichols Boulevard N.E.** along edge of Sacajawea Park. Bear left with Nichols Boulevard as State Route 432 merges from the right.

20.3 Turn left across sidewalk as Hemlock Street goes right. Cross Lake Sacajawea on pedestrian footbridge. Picnic area with tables, water, rest rooms, shade trees, and lawn at other edge of park; picnic lunch stop. After lunch, turn left on **Kessler Boulevard.**

20.5 Bear right on **25 Avenue** and immediately turn right on **Hudson Street.** Follow Hudson through edge of downtown Longview.

21.9 Turn left on **3rd Avenue (State Route 411)** at traffic light. Enter Kelso at mile 22.6.

22.8 Turn right on **West Main Street** and cross the Cowlitz River. Pedestrian walkway available. Road name changes to **Allen Street.**

23.0 Immediately after crossing bridge, turn left and walk bikes across Allen Street and continue on **First Avenue.** (No left turn for vehicles.) *Note: Bakery one block farther on Allen Street.*

23.6 Turn left on **Pacific Highway North,** a narrow, concrete two-lane roadway. *Note: Optional left turn on Cowlitz Gardens Road at mile 24.7, which rejoins 0.5 mile beyond.* Road climbs hill alongside masonry-lined cut on hillside. Main-line tracks tunnel underneath; logging railroad crosses river and goes overhead on trestle. Go under I-5 at mile 25.6 and continue alongside highway.

26.8 Turn left on **Pleasant Hill Road** and cross I-5 on 1975 overpass.

32.0 Turn left on **Huntington Avenue** and cross railroad tracks on high bridge. Enter Castle Rock. End of tour at Lions Pride Park at mile 32.7.

INTERSTATE TOURS

138 LONGVIEW–SKAMOKAWA

STARTING POINT: Intersection of Hemlock Street and Kessler Boulevard by rest rooms of Sacajawea Park in Longview. Take exit 36 (State Route 432) from I-5 toward Longview. Turn right on Oregon Avenue at traffic light where S.R. 432 ends, and then immediately turn left on Kessler Boulevard. Follow Kessler to Hemlock Street by rest rooms. Park along Kessler by Sacajawea Park.

DISTANCE: Total 67 to 80 miles: first day, 32 to 49 miles; second day, 32 to 45 miles.
TERRAIN: Flat terrain and strenuous hills.
TOTAL CUMULATIVE ELEVATION GAIN: 3300 feet: first day, 2200 feet; second day, 1100 feet.
RECOMMENDED TIME OF YEAR: Any season.

RECOMMENDED STARTING TIME: 9 A.M.
ALLOW: 2 days.
POINTS OF INTEREST
Beaver Falls
Westport-Puget Island Ferry
Julia Butler Hansen Wildlife Refuge for Columbian white-tailed deer

ELEVATION PROFILE

When Lewis and Clark explored the Northwest Territory of the United States of America at the beginning of the nineteenth century, the only highways were the nation's great waterways. The Columbia River was the final such waterway leading them to the Pacific Ocean. Today the lower Columbia is still a major transportation route. Huge ocean-going ships ply the deep, free-flowing waters where canoes and longboats transported the early American explorers in 1805. Many ships tie up at Longview to receive cargoes of aluminum, paper products, and Orient-bound logs, while other ships continue upriver to Portland. This tour explores the Washington and Oregon shores of this great river and crosses it twice, once via the small Wahkiakum County ferryboat *M. V. Wahkiakum* (what else!), and again on the return via the high, arching Longview Bridge.

The tour begins well away from the water's edge, taking to the hills on the Washington side in order to escape the narrow, nondescript shoulders and heavy traffic of Washington's State Route 4. Eventually the backroads run out, and the route follows the highway along one of the few stretches with

181

waterscape views, diverting again for the seclusion of Spruce Creek Valley. All valleys end in a summit somewhere, however, and this valley is no exception. The high divide gives way to the Beaver Creek drainage, where young Douglas-fir plantations host deer, elk, and the ethereal hoot of the blue grouse. An exhilarating downhill run levels out by the Beaver Creek Trout Hatchery, followed by a relaxing ride along the Elochoman River.

The Julia Butler Hansen Wildlife Refuge, encompassing several thousand acres and three islands in the Columbia River, is a treat for animal and bird watchers. Waterfowl inhabit the sluggish sloughs, while goldfinches, game birds, elk, and deer cavort about the grassy meadows. Navigation aids for river traffic decorate the roadside as the islands part for a brief riverscape. A late evening or early morning return through the wildlife refuge almost always reaps rewards for the alert watcher.

Just past sleepy little Skamokawa (pronounced "Skam-**ah**-ka-way"), Wahkiakum County's Skamokawa Vista Park features campsites with all the usual amenities along the Columbia River. A motel, hotel, and bed-and-breakfast places in Cathlamet and on Puget Island offer more expensive accommodations.

The ride out of Cathlamet across the mid-river islands is flat, and roads along the levees beckon for scenic detours. With nothing to block it, however, the wind occasionally comes whistling up the river across the flat islands, increasing the motive effort.

The short ride across the river on the *M. V. Wahkiakum* is yet another adventure. The meandering sloughs are reminiscent of the bayous of the Mississippi Delta. Great ships go rumbling by in the main channel. Traffic- and wind-generated swells mandate the stabilization of bicycles by hooking handlebars over railings.

As the tour leaves Westport, short stretches of highway shoulder are interspersed with offshoots of almost-forgotten Old U.S. 30. Monoclonal plantations of the shiny-leaved hybrid poplar, covering hundreds of acres, are a recent silvicultural pursuit supplying the paper pulp industry. In Clatskanie (pronounced "**Clat**-skan-eye"), cafes offer early lunch fare, fuel for ascending the Beaver Creek Valley. Exposed volcanic rock along the roadsides tells of the area's fiery geologic history. The waterfall on Beaver Creek is not grandiose, as falls go, but the vertical fall from an overhanging ledge is impressive. Columbian white-tailed deer, a staple of the early explorers' diet, still roam the forest, occasionally bounding across the road in front of startled bicyclists. Wildflowers bloom along the roadside to round out an idyllic scene.

Near the summit, bicyclists have the choice of a rapid descent along the highway with scenic turnouts, or a more leisurely set of switchbacks through the forest on the old highway. Either way leads to the approach to the Longview bridge over the Columbia River. The high, arching bridge, too-narrow walkway, and lack of shoulder all keep the adrenalin flowing. The view from the bridge summit is breathtaking, affording far-ranging inspection of port activities and river traffic below.

Once off the bridge on the Washington side, the route leaves the highway, returning quickly to the starting point in Longview's Sacajawea Park.

MILEAGE LOG

FIRST DAY

0.0 Starting from Kessler Boulevard and Hemlock Street by Sacajawea Park rest rooms, head north on **Kessler Boulevard.**

0.7 Turn hard left on **Ocean Beach Highway (State Route 4)** as Kessler Boulevard ends.

0.9 Turn right on **Pacific Way.** Grocery on right at 2.4.

6.0 Turn right and uphill on **Coal Creek Road** as Pacific Way ends.

6.2 Turn left downhill on **Harmony Drive** toward Eufala Heights. Cross Coal Creek and begin long climb.

7.7 Bear left and uphill on **Stella Road** as Harmony Drive is marked Dead End. Top a summit at 9.5 and begin undulating descent.

11.7 Bear right on **Fall Creek Road** as Stella Road ends. Ascend to a summit and descend steeply.

13.2 Turn hard left on **Germany Creek Road** as Fall Creek Road ends.

15.1 Turn right on **State Route 4** as Germany Creek Road ends. Viewpoints along Columbia River.

17.8 Turn right on **Mill Creek Road** and begin gradual climb along scenic Mill Creek.

18.9 Bear left across creek on **Spruce Creek Road** as Mill Creek Road is marked Dead End.

19.5 Turn right on **Cathlamet Road** toward Cathlamet as Spruce Creek Road is marked Dead End. Enter Wahkiakum County at mile 20.2. Go over summit at mile 23.7 and begin long, winding descent as road name changes to **Beaver Creek Road.**

28.1 Cross Elochoman River and turn left on **State Route 407** as Beaver Creek Road ends by Beaver Creek Trout Hatchery. Public fishing access on left along Elochoman River.

31.8 Turn right on **State Route 4** as S.R. 407 ends. *Note: Tour may be shortened 13 miles by turning left on S.R. 4 to Cathlamet.*

33.1 Cross Elochoman River and turn left on **Steamboat Slough Road** into the Julia Butler Hansen National Wildlife Refuge for white-tailed deer. Proceed on a narrow, paved road through refuge, along sloughs and main channel of Columbia River. *Note: Strong winds may be encountered along exposed stretches.*

38.2 Cross Brooks Slough and stop at State Route 4 in Skamokawa; cafe and grocery. *Note: For bicycle camping facilities, turn left on S.R. 4 for 0.2 mile to Wahkiakum County's Skamokawa Vista Park.* Return along Steamboat Slough Road through refuge.

43.3 Turn right on **State Route 4** as Steamboat Slough Road ends. Cross Elochoman River.

45.3 Turn right on **State Route 409** through Cathlamet (cafe, grocery, hotel, motel, B & B's) toward ferry. Continue across bridge to Little Island at 45.8, and across Birnie Slough to Puget Island at 47.5. Board ferry at mile 49.0; ferry departs hourly from 7:15 A.M. to 5:15 P.M. and then not again until 11:30 P.M. Disembark ferry in Westport, Oregon.

SCALE OF MILES

0   1   2   3

SECOND DAY

0.0 Continue through Westport on **Ferry Road**.

0.4 Turn left on **U.S. 30**; motel, restaurant, and grocery. Enter Columbia County at 1.2.

2.1 Turn right on unmarked side road, which bends left and becomes **Old Highway 30**.

3.2 Turn right on **U.S. 30** toward Clatskanie. Skirt high bluffs and rock quarry.

4.2 Go past rock piles and turn right on unmarked side road, then left at T junction on **Old Highway 30**.

8.0 Turn right on **U.S. 30** as old highway ends. Beaver Boat Ramp (public toilets) on left at 10.0; Flippin House National Historic Museum uphill to right at 10.1.

10.2 Turn left at traffic light on **Nehalem Street** in Clatskanie; cafes, grocery; motels 0.2 mile farther along U.S. 30.

10.4 Turn left at stop sign on **N.W. 5th Street** toward Port Westward as Nehalem Street ends. Road is shortly renamed **Old U.S. 30**.

11.1 Bear right with Old U.S. 30 as Depot Road goes left. Road is promptly renamed **Beaver Falls Road**.

13.4 Turn right at wye with Beaver Falls Road as Mayger Road goes left. Pass overlook to Beaver Creek Falls (listen for it) at 16.8; dirt track leads right to ford at top of falls at 17.0.

20.2 Turn left on **U.S. 30**. *Note: To avoid recrossing highway, use left shoulder.*

20.8 Bear left toward Alston on old highway; Alston Country Store at 21.5.

21.5 Cross U.S. 30 and continue toward Vernonia on **Old Rainier Road**. Hudson-Parcher Park (Columbia County) on the right on Larson Road at 24.0. *Note: To descend hill on highway, turn left on Larson, then right on U.S. 30. Bear right toward Longview at bottom of hill.* Continue over summit and down long, winding grade. Views of Columbia River and Longview Bridge.

27.0 Turn sharp left on **Washington Way**.

27.6 Turn right on **Rockcrest Street** past gas station and grocery, then left on **U.S. 30**. Immediately bear right at interchange toward Longview and Seattle; cross Columbia River and enter Longview, Washington.

29.6 Get into left turn lane at traffic light and turn left on **Alabama Street**.

30.0 Turn right on **20th Avenue**. Cross Nichols Boulevard and Lake Sacajawea.

30.3 Turn left on **Kessler Boulevard** on far side of bridge.

31.0 End of tour by rest rooms in Sacajawea Park.

139 COLUMBIA GORGE

STARTING POINT: Vancouver, Washington, Amtrak depot. By automobile, take exit 1C from I-5 and head west on 14th Street. Turn left on Washington Street, right on Evergreen Boulevard, right on Jefferson Street to 11th Street, then left on 11th Street to depot parking area. Notify station agent of long-term parking intentions.

ALTERNATIVE STARTING POINT: Portland Airport parking area. By automobile, take Airport Way exit from I-205 just south of Columbia River Bridge. Proceed toward airport and park in Economy Parking Area. By bicycle, head east on Airport Way 2.6 miles to its end at N.E. 138th Avenue, then left on 138th 0.2 mile to Marine Drive to join main route.

DISTANCE: Full tour, 318 miles; minimum daily mileages from 12 to 45. Shorter loops from 60 to 90 miles.
TERRAIN: Flat, moderate, hilly, and mountainous; 5 miles of gravel road.
TOTAL CUMULATIVE ELEVATION GAIN: Full tour, 12,000 feet; daily totals from 50 to 2600 feet.
RECOMMENDED TIME OF YEAR: June through October.
ALLOW: 7 to 10 days for full tour; shorter loops, 1 to 3 days.
RECOMMENDED ADDITIONAL GUIDEBOOKS:
1) Plumb, Gregory. *Waterfalls of the Pacific Northwest*. Seattle, WA: Writing Works, 1983.
2) Jones, Philip and Henderson, Jean. *Bicycling the Backroads of Northwest Oregon*. Seattle, WA: The Mountaineers, 1992.
3) Allen, John E. *The Magnificent Gateway, A Layman's Guide to the Geology of the Columbia River Gorge*. Forest Grove, OR: Timber Press, 1984.

POINTS OF INTEREST

OREGON
Portland Women's Forum State Park
Vista House at Crown Point
Waterfalls: 5 visible from road, 15 or more accessible by short hikes
Bonneville Dam Locks, Bradford Island Visitor Center and Fish Hatchery
Rowena Overlook
Historic buildings in The Dalles
The Dalles Dam guided tours
Celilo Indian Village

WASHINGTON
Maryhill Museum
Stonehenge reproduction
Museum and state park observatory in Goldendale
Ice House Park near Klickitat
Klickitat River scenery
Bonneville Dam Visitor Center
Rafting on Klickitat and White Salmon rivers
Ice caves
Mountain views
Mountain wildflowers
Carson Hot Springs
Beacon Rock
Pendleton Woolen Mills

Barring adverse winds, and using the primary highways on both sides of the Columbia Gorge, it is possible to travel round trip by bicycle from Camas to Maryhill in two days. If that is your objective, read no further; you don't need this book.

ELEVATION PROFILES

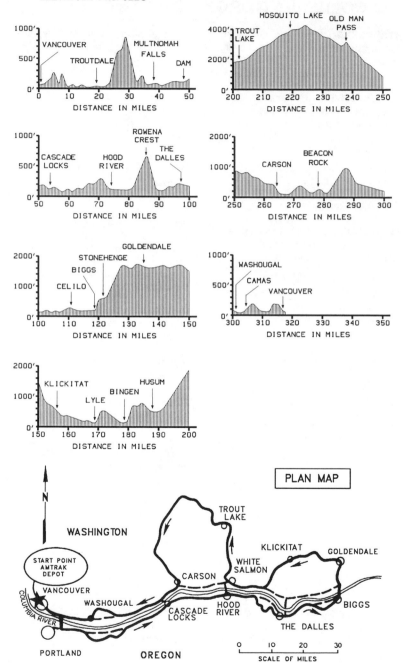

PLAN MAP

188

As implied by the preceding Points of Interest, this tour offers a spectacular mix of natural scenery, waterfalls, wildflowers, cultural features, diverse recreational opportunities, and history. As a bicycling vacation route, it is one of the best, featuring a choice of accommodations from rudimentary campgrounds to expensive resort hotels, with several bed-and-breakfast opportunities thrown in.

Three bridges cross the Columbia River between the ends of this gorge tour, offering several options for shorter tours. The mileage log, rather than being split arbitrarily into day sections, is cumulative for the full tour, allowing the bicycle tourist to adjust the route and stopping points easily to his or her own liking.

For the botany or bird buff, the extreme variety of this tour, from sea level to high mountains and from rain forest to desert, presents a challenge to identify an unusually broad range of flora and fauna. The amateur geologist is presented with strikingly vivid layering of sedimentary and igneous formations, mountain folding, and massive earth slides. Even the amateur astronomer may have his day (or night) at the Goldendale Observatory. Cultivated fruit in season along the route includes cherries, apricots, peaches, and apples. Each major feature — waterfall, hydroelectric dam, museum, wild river, ice cave, soda spring, hot spring, mountain view, and manufacturing plant tour — would be a reasonable objective on its own. This tour combines them all.

As the tour leaves the Amtrak station in Vancouver, it traverses low-traffic side streets. A very brief exposure to the busy one-way grid is followed by a

High riders

tour through old Fort Vancouver, with its officers quarters and parade grounds. Following the old Evergreen Highway, the route plays leapfrog with the newer State Route 14 and crosses the Columbia River to Oregon on a unique bikeway down the center of Interstate 205, with traffic roaring by on either side. On the Oregon side, a grade-separated bikeway along the Columbia River provides a placid waterscape away from all traffic concerns. Eventually the route is forced inland, first along the Sandy River, then up over headlands for scenic views of the Columbia River Gorge. A steep plunge down switchbacks from the Vista House leads to a myriad of waterfalls over the basalt cliffs formed by the geologically recent lava flows and the cataclysmic carvings of the Columbia River.

Leaving spectacular Multnomah Falls behind, the tour proceeds along short stretches of the Interstate 84 freeway shoulder, broken by a side trip to the Bonneville Dam Visitor Center with its displays and tours, and by sections of old U.S. 30 through Cascade Locks and Hood River. The tour then climbs through orchards and lava beds to Rowena Crest with its breathtaking views. At The Dalles, another dam tour is offered, with a tram ride from the visitor center to a delightful park, powerhouse, and dam.

From Celilo to Biggs, the old highway parallels the interstate up the gorge, with the prevailing westerly tailwinds assisting high-gear cranking. These same winds, however, can pose significant crosswind difficulty crossing the bridge to Maryhill. At Maryhill, a fruit stand provides seasonal fuel for the climb to the Stonehenge replica and the ensuing long grind up the highway shoulder to the Goldendale plateau. Not far beyond the summit, the old highway appears again, and provides a low-traffic experience over hill and dale to Goldendale.

From Goldendale, the route bends west and winds across the plateau through farmlands and forest, eventually diving down into the Klickitat Canyon with spectacular views and exciting switchbacks. But be careful: there are no shoulders and no guardrails to protect cyclists from the steep drop-offs. The rest of the route down the canyon is very scenic, but without the excitement of exposure.

Beyond the Klickitat Canyon, a stretch of highway must once again be negotiated, this time against the prevailing westerlies. Soon the town of Bingen appears, and the long, scenic climb begins up the White Salmon River, through farmland and forest to Trout Lake, the lava-tube ice caves, Langfield Falls, and unusual views of Mt. Adams, Mt. Rainier, and Mt. St. Helens. In early summer the mountain wildflowers put on a spectacular display. Eventually the summit is gained, and the long downhill run begins, interrupted once by a short climb to Old Man Pass on the Wind River Road, after which the descent seems to go on forever.

After going through Carson, the route proceeds west on the highway through Stevenson, stopping briefly at the north end of Bonneville Dam for another powerhouse and fish ladder tour. The hike up the Beacon Rock trail is spectacular with its cantilevered, switchbacking walkways to a narrow summit overlooking many miles of the Columbia River.

Soon the route leaves the highway again, following a narrow, winding backroad on a short ascent to a low summit, then proceeding down the long, gradual, winding descent to Washougal and the enticing Pendleton Woolen Mills factory and thrift shop. A short stretch of city traffic is traversed to Camas, where the old, bypassed Evergreen Highway follows the Columbia River back to the starting point at Vancouver.

MILEAGE LOG

0.0 From the Vancouver Amtrak depot, head north through parking lot, cross spur track, and bear right on **West 11th Street**.

0.7 Turn right on **Washington Street** (one way), then get into left lane and almost immediately turn left on **Evergreen Boulevard** and cross I-5 on overpass. *Note: Fort Vancouver Way goes right to Fort Vancouver Historical Museum at mile 1.2.*

4.5 Bear left on **Slaret Avenue** as Evergreen is barred by a freeway exit, then turn right on **S.E. Middle Way**.

5.3 Turn right at stop sign on **S.E. Lieser Road**. Cross State Route 14 on overpass and turn left on **Frontage Road** toward Camas on other side.

5.6 Bear right on **S.E. 88th Avenue**.

5.7 Turn left on **S.E. Evergreen Highway**.

6.8 Turn left on **S.E. Ellsworth Road**.

6.9 Turn right on **S.E. 23rd Street** for 0.2 mile, then turn left through bollards on bikeway. Cross I-205 bridge in central bike lane, fenced off from traffic by concrete and steel railings. Descend ramp at far end of bridge.

9.9 Turn left toward Marine Drive as Bike Route divides at a wye.

10.1 Turn right on **Marine Drive** and follow marked bikeway on shoulder. Grade-separated bikeway begins at mile 10.9. *Note: Route from*

Portland Airport joins from right at mile 11.5. Cross Marine Drive at 11.6 and continue along the Columbia River on a grade-separated bikeway. Rejoin **Marine Drive** at 13.5.

15.0 Turn right on bike route alongside Blue Lake Park Drive. Cross roadway and continue on grade-separated bikeway. Bikeway ends at 17.1; continue along **Marine Drive**.

17.8 Turn left with Bike Route on **N. Frontage Road** as Marine Drive continues under I-84. *Note: Motels and cafe in Troutdale on other side of underpass.*

18.2 Turn right with Bike Route under I-84 on **Graham road**. Go through traffic light and continue uphill past shopping center.

18.5 Turn left at traffic light on **Columbia Boulevard** toward Scenic Highway and Corbett. Continue through Troutdale business district.

19.3 Cross the Sandy River and turn right on **Crown Point Highway** toward Corbett; historical marker. *Note: Park Street goes right across the Sandy River at mile 21.8 toward Gresham and Oxbow County Park; nine miles, camping. Next campground at mile 41.2.* Dabney State Park (day use only) on right at mile 22.2. Grocery and delicatessen in Springdale at mile 23.2.

23.5 Bear right with Scenic Highway toward Multnomah Falls. Grocery in Corbett at 27.3. Portland Women's Forum State Park on left at mile 27.7; memorial to Sam Hill, road builder. Vista House on Crown Point at mile 29.0. Talbot State Park (day use only) at mile 31.2.

31.5 La Tourell Falls on right; walking trail to falls continues back through Talbot State Park and returns to Scenic Highway. Falls in Shepperd's Dell State Park on right at 32.7. Bridal Veil State Park on left at 33.6; 0.5-mile trail to falls. Wahkeena Falls on right at 37.0.

37.6 Multnomah Falls on right; trail to falls viewpoint and Upper Falls; cafe and restaurant. *Note: Oneonta Trail #424 goes right at mile 39.6 to*

Oneonta Falls, Triple Falls, and Upper Horsetail Falls; recommended side trip if bicycles are locked to trees ¼ mile up trail. Oneonta Botanical Area on right at 39.7. Horsetail Falls at mile 40.1; Ainsworth State Park (camping) on right at mile 41.1.

41.3 Bear right toward Hood River and I-84 East.

41.6 Bear right on **Frontage Road**. Trail to Elowah Falls goes right at mile 43.8.

43.9 Join **I-84** and continue on shoulder. Beacon Rock appears across Columbia River. Narrow bridge at mile 45.2.

46.3 Bear right on **Exit 40** toward Bonneville Dam. Turn left at stop sign and follow arrows to visitor center. Be careful of rails in roadway by powerhouse.

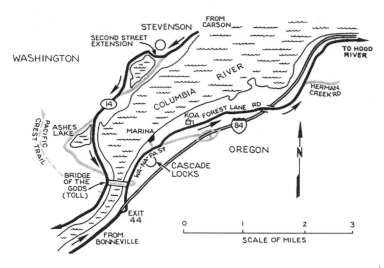

47.9   Bradford Island Visitor Center. Tour visitor center and return to I-84. *Note: Side road goes right to fish hatchery at mile 49.0.*

49.3   Go under I-84 and take up-ramp to **I-84 East**. Go through lighted tunnel at mile 50.3.

52.5   Take **Exit 44** (**U.S. 30 East**) toward Cascade Locks. *Note: Tour may be short-cut by taking grating-decked toll bridge across Columbia River here.* Continue through town on **WA-NA-PA Street** (motels and cafes). Cascade Locks Marina, museum, and Amtrak station on the left on Portage Road at mile 53.5

53.9   Turn left on **Forest Lane Road** toward Airport and Industrial Park. KOA Campground on the left at mile 54.9.

"Look at the neat little lights along this road."

55.9 Cross bridge over I-84 and bear left toward Herman Creek Road. Herman Creek Campground (Forest Service) on the right at mile 56.3.

56.8 Bear left toward I-84 as Herman Creek Road goes right. Continue on shoulder of **I-84**.

64.5 Bear right into highway rest area (Starvation Creek State Park). Memorial to construction of Columbia River Highway, begun here in 1912. Picnic area and trails to Starvation Creek Falls and Cabin Creek Falls. Return to I-84 at mile 64.7. *Note: Exit 56 goes right at mile 65.9 to Viento State Park; camping.*

71.8 Bear right on **Exit 62** toward West Hood River. Continue on **W. Cascade Avenue** downhill into Hood River. *Note: For a more-than-you-can-eat breakfast by reservation, turn left at stop sign, cross overpass, then left on Westcliff Drive to Columbia Gorge Hotel. Lower-priced motels nearby.*

73.0 Turn right on **1st Street**; Amtrak station is downhill on the left. Climb hill and turn left on **State Street**. Cross Hood River.

73.4 Turn left on **State Route 35** toward I-84 and toll bridge.

73.6 Turn right at entrance to **I-84 East** toward Celilo, and continue on shoulder. *Note: S.R. 35 continues across Columbia River to Bingen; possible tour shortcut.*

79.0 Take **Exit 69** and bear right on **U.S. Hwy 30** toward Scenic Loop and Mosier. Grocery at mile 79.4; cherry orchards at 80.9.

85.9 Turn right into Rowena Crest Viewpoint for overlook. Return to U.S. 30 at 86.3. Tom McCall Preserve on left at next bend; Mayer State Park at bottom of hill at 88.3. Enter The Dalles; cafes and restaurants.

96.8 Turn left with U.S. 30 on **Webber Street**, go under I-84, then right on **2nd Street**. Tourist Information Center in old Wasco County Courthouse in The Dalles at 96.9 (maps and lists of historic structures in The Dalles). All services in The Dalles.

97.0 Turn right, then left on **3rd Street** with one-way grid.

97.8 Rejoin **2nd Street** with U.S. 30. Visitor information center on the left.

98.3 Keep right with U.S. 30 toward State Route 197.

99.5 Turn left on **State Route 197** toward freeway and Yakima. Cross overpass and turn right on **Bret Clodfelter Way** toward Dalles Dam.

100.8   Stop at The Dalles Dam Visitor Center for free tram ride and dam tour, then return to S.R. 197.

101.7   Turn left on **State Route 197**, cross overpass, and turn left on entrance to **I-84 East**. *Note: S.R. 197 goes north across Columbia River to Washington's Horsethief Lake State Park; camping and possible shortcut to tour.* Exit 88 at mile 103.6 is signed for Dalles Dam, but entrance to dam area is blocked by a locked gate.

111.9   Bear right on **Exit 97** (**State Route 206**), then turn right with S.R. 206 as left goes under freeway to Celilo Park; rest rooms, water, picnic tables, green lawns, views of Columbia River.

112.0   Turn left with S.R. 206 East as right goes to Celilo Indian Village; tourist displays, salmon bake on second weekend in April. Cross Deschutes River at 115.0 and pass Deschutes River State Park; camping, picnicking.

116.7 Continue on **U.S. 30** as S.R. 206 turns right.

119.6 Turn left on **U.S. 97** in Biggs; grocery, motels, cafes. Cross Columbia River into Washington State. *Note: Strong crosswinds are common on bridge.*

120.6 Turn right toward Maryhill State Park. *Note: No group camp, no reservations; campground full every night from mid-June to mid-September.* Continue past park on old roadway toward Stonehenge.

121.6 Turn left toward Stonehenge at stop sign in Maryhill by old church. Cherry and apricot orchards.

122.6 Turn left by souvenir shop into Stonehenge entrance. Stonehenge replica at 122.7. Tour the replica, view monument to Sam Hill, and head back out to entrance.

122.8 Turn left toward State Route 14 at entrance.

123.4 Turn left on (Washington) **State Route 14**. Join **U.S. 97** as it comes uphill on the left at mile 124.4.

125.0 Turn right (uphill) with U.S. 97. *Note: Maryhill Museum is 2.6 miles farther west on S.R. 14; open 9 A.M. to 5 P.M.* Mountain viewpoint at 129.7; top of grade (elevation 1700 feet).

131.6 Turn left, then right on **S. Columbus Avenue** as Hector Road goes right. Enter Goldendale.

134.9 Turn left on **State Route 142 (West Broadway)** in Goldendale. Groceries, cafes, motels, museum; Washington State Park Observatory open to public Wednesday through Sunday evenings. Go through community of Blockhouse at mile 141.3. *Note: Glenwood Road goes right at mile 145.6 to Glenwood, 24 miles; Trout Lake, 42 miles; 1200-foot climb out of Klickitat Gorge to Glenwood.* Start down long, steep, scenic hill with switchbacks and no guardrails at 146.6. Department of Wildlife Conservation Park on left at 154.0; soda spring, pit toilets, Klickitat River. Town of Klickitat at mile 156.2; cafe, grocery, hotel. Continue down Klickitat Canyon.

169.4 Turn right on **State Route 14** as S.R. 142 ends. *Note: Grocery and cafe in Lyle, ¼ mile left on S.R. 14.* Chamberlin Lake Rest Area on the left at mile 171.3.

179.0 Continue on S.R. 14 in Bingen as State Route 141 goes right and uphill on Oak Street; grocery, cafes, campground, park, motel, B & B, winery, Amtrak station. *Note: Turning right on S.R. 141 shortens the route by 0.2 mile but is much steeper, adding 150 feet of elevation gain.* Toll bridge goes left to Hood River at mile 180.4.

181.9 Turn right on **State Route 141 Alternate** just before S.R. 14 crosses the White Salmon River. Climb through forest on a moderate grade.

184.1 Turn left on **State Route 141** as S.R. 141 Alternate ends at stop sign. *Note: Side road goes left 0.5 mile to Northwestern Lake at mile 186.0; camping, food concession, raft trips.* Husum Cafe at 188.0;

BZ Corners grocery at 192.0. Go through Trout Lake at 203.3; cafe, grocery, B & B's, sleeping rooms in back of general store, camping in county park. Ranger station at 204.1.

205.0   Turn right on **Trout Lake Creek Road** (**Forest Road 88**). *Note: Ice caves picnic area and campground 5.1 miles farther on S.R. 141 and Forest Road 24.*

217.8   Continue on **Forest Road 8851** as Road 88 turns right at Big Tire Junction. *Note: Langfield Falls trailhead is 0.1 mile right on Road 88.* Cross Pacific Crest Trail at mile 220.5, elevation 3900 feet; go by Mosquito Lake at 220.6.

221.1   Bear left on **Forest Road 24** as Road 8851 forks right.

224.5   Bear right on **Forest Road 30** as Road 24 turns left up a steep hill and turns to gravel. *Note: Road 580 goes left at mile 225.9 up steep hill to Mt. St. Helens viewpoint with pit toilets, but just as good a viewpoint is 0.5 mile farther along Forest Road 30.* Pavement ends at mile 227.2 for 5.2 miles of gravel surface.

232.5   Turn left on **Wind River Road** (paved!) as Road 30 (Lone Butte Road) ends. Watch for logging trucks. Sno-park site with pit toilet and picnic table on the right at mile 235.9. Crest of Old Man Pass (3000 ft.) at mile 237.4; sno-park rest rooms. Paradise Creek Campground on the left at mile 242.2; campsites and pit toilets but no potable water.

248.5   Turn right on **Mineral Springs Road**.

248.9   Cross Wind River and turn left on **Little Soda Springs Road**; unpaved, but hard-packed old railroad grade.

251.9   Continue on Little Soda Springs Road (now paved) as Szydlo Road joins from the right.

255.4   Turn left on **Hemlock Pass Road** as Trout Creek Road continues.

255.8   Turn right on **Wind River Road** at stop sign in Stabler. *Note: St. Martin Hot Springs hotel, motel, cafe, and spa left 1.3 miles on Hot Springs Road in Carson at mile 263.5.*

264.5   Turn right on **State Route 14** as Wind River Road ends. Enter Stevenson at mile 267.3; cafes, grocery, motel.

267.8   Bear right on **Rock Creek Drive** in Stevenson (see map, page 194) and ride past Skamania County Fairgrounds and Rock Creek Park. Skamania Lodge resort and golf links uphill on the right.

269.2   Turn right on **State Route 14** as Rock Creek Drive ends. Historical markers at 270.1, 270.7, and 271.8. Bridge of the Gods (toll, grating-decked) goes left to Cascade Locks at 270.7. Cross Pacific Crest Trail at 271.0.

272.7   Turn left into Bonneville Dam North Shore Visitor Center. After dam visit, bear left (west) on **Dam Access Road**. (See map, page 193.)

274.1   Turn right toward highway as road is marked No Outlet. Cross State Route 14, go under railroad trestle, and turn left on **Cascade Drive**.

274.7   Turn right on **Evergreen Drive** just before Cascade Drive goes under State Route 14.

275.8   Turn right on State Route 14 toward Vancouver. Beacon Rock State Park rest area, Beacon Rock trail, and campground at 278.0. Cafe and grocery in Skamania at 279.9.

285.9   Turn right on **Krogstad Road** shortly after passing lane ends on uphill grade.

286.1   Continue right and uphill as Krogstad forks left down to S.R. 14.

286.7   Turn right at stop sign and continue uphill. Cross Salmon Falls Road at 287.5, just short of summit. Skamania County Prindle Park (day use only) at 289.8.

290.7   Cross Washougal River and turn left by grocery toward Washougal on **Washougal River Road**. Enter Clark County at mile 291.7.

300.7   Turn right on **E Street** at traffic light in Washougal. *Note: Pendleton Woolen Mills at 17th and A streets.* Enter Camas at mile 301.7, where road is renamed **N.E. 3rd Avenue**.

303.5   Turn right with thoroughfare on **N.E. Adams Street** and pass Crown Zellerbach paper mill.

303.6   Turn left with thoroughfare on **N.E. 6th Avenue**.

304.7 Turn hard left with **N.W. 6th Avenue** toward Washougal at highway
interchange as the road ahead becomes a divided highway. Cross
overpass with **S.W. 6th Avenue** and continue on old highway.

317.9 Bear left on **S.E. Evergreen Highway** toward State Fish Hatchery
as road forks. Fish hatchery and historical monument at 310.9. *Note:
Bike route goes right at 311.7 on S.E. Ellsworth and S.E. 23rd Street
across I-205 bridge to Marine Drive, Portland Airport, and alternative
start point.*

312.8 Turn left with bike route on **S.E. Chelsea**, then right at stop sign on
Riverside Drive.

313.4 Turn left at stop sign, then bear right across overpass on **Columbia
Way**.

313.8 Turn left on **E. Evergreen Boulevard**. Cross I-5 on overpass in
Vancouver at mile 316.5.

317.3 Turn right on **Jefferson Street** as Evergreen is blocked by Exit Only
signs, then left on **11th Street** to the end of the tour at the Amtrak
terminal at mile 317.6.

ALPHABETICAL INDEX

MILEAGE INDEX – DAY TOURS

MILEAGE INDEX–OVERNIGHT AND MULTI-DAY TOURS

WASHINGTON STATE PARKS

PARK	TOUR NO.	PARK	TOUR NO.
Battle Ground Lake	134	Millersylvania	47, 48, 49, 50, 51, 119, 120
Belfair	108	Nolte	8, 97
Federation Forest	105	Ocean City	110, 111
Flaming Geyser	7, 97	Pacific Beach	111
Fort Canby	133	Pacific Pines	133
Jarrell Cove	109	Palmer-Kanaskat	8, 97
Kopachuck	94, 95	Paradise Point	134
Lake Sylvia	116	Penrose Point	95
Leadbetter Point	133	Rainbow Falls	132
Lewis and Clark	128, 129, 130	Schafer	46, 114
Loomis Lake	133	Seaquest	131, 132, 136
Manchester	44, 95	Tolmie	118
Maryhill	139	Twanoh	106

TOURS WITH BED-AND-BREAKFAST ACCOMMODATIONS

TOUR NO. NAME	B & B LOCATION	PHONE NO.
94 Southworth–Gig Harbor	Gig Harbor	(206) 851-8654
95 Southworth–Longbranch	Port Orchard	(206) 871-5582
98 Enumclaw–Auburn	Enumclaw	(206) 825-6381
105 Mt. Rainier	Ashford	(206) 569-2339
	Eatonville	(206) 832-6506
107 Mason Lake–Grapeview	Allyn	(206) 275-5378
108 Belfair–Tahuya	Belfair	(206) 275-2676
110 Ocean Shores	Ocean Shores	(206) 289-3036
112 Aberdeen–Hoquiam–Wishkah	Hoquiam	(206) 533-2320
116 Oakville–Brooklyn–Montesano	Montesano	(206) 249-3453
118 Priest Point–Tolmie State Park	Olympia	(206) 754-0389
	by Tolmie Park	(206) 459-1676
119 Millersylvania–Delphi–Olympia	Olympia	(206) 754-0389
133 Long Beach Peninsula	Seaview	(206) 642-4177
134 Lewis River	Battle Ground	(206) 686-3029
138 Longview–Skamokawa	Cathlamet	(206) 795-3624
	Cathlamet	(206) 795-3030
	Puget Island	(206) 849-4108
139 Columbia Gorge	Glenwood	(509) 364-3488
	Hood River, OR	(503) 386-5566
	Husum	(509) 493-3024
	Stevenson	(509) 427-7070
	The Dalles, OR	(503) 296-2793
	Trout Lake	(509) 395-2786
	White Salmon	(509) 493-2335

TOUR JUNCTIONS

Note: Tours 1 through 54 are found in *Bicycling the Backroads Around Puget Sound,* and tours 55 through 93 are found in *Bicycling the Backroads of Northwest Washington.* Seattle, WA: The Mountaineers.

"But it will save four miles and almost 2000 feet in elevation."